STRETFORD

AN ILLUSTRATED HISTORY

STRETFORD

AN ILLUSTRATED HISTORY

VICKI MASTERSON AND KAREN CLIFF

irst published in Great Britain byThe Breedon Books Publishing Company Limited
Breedon House, 44 Friar Gate, Derby, DE1 1DA. 1999

This paperback edition published in Great Britain in 2015 by DB Publishing, an imprint of
JMD Media Ltd

ISBN 978-1-78091-499-2

Printed and bound in the UK by Copytech (UK) Ltd Peterborough

CONTENTS

INTRODUCTION

STRETFORD is now part of the Metropolitan Borough of Trafford. It is situated on the north side of the River Mersey and was once in the county of Lancashire. In 1933 Stretford was given its Charter and in 1974 it became part of the Borough of Trafford. Stretford lies to the south-west of Manchester on the Roman road from Chester to the city. Over the last three centuries Stretford has undergone dramatic changes, from a rural, farming community to an urban, industrialised centre that forms the basis of the town we know today. This new history charts the course of this development with the use of photographs and the mine of information to be found in the archives of Trafford Local Studies.

Most of the land around Stretford was owned by the de Traffords. They were the owners of Trafford Hall and the surrounding parkland and have a noble past stretching back generations. We can only imagine the way of life in the days before the industrialisation of the area, and the chapter on landowners helps us picture the old Stretford and explains how the family lost much of its standing in the country on its conversion from Protestantism to the Catholic faith. When the Bridgewater Canal was dug the estate was cut off, and, by the time the Manchester Ship Canal was constructed, the whole park had become unviable. The de Traffords sold up and Trafford Park changed from a peaceful deer park and hall to one of the biggest industrial complexes in Europe. We will trace the history of the park from rural retreat to industrial giant.

The other large landowner and entrepreneur was John Rylands from whose philanthropy the area benefited immensely. He was responsible for the building of many gracious buildings, including the now demolished Longford Hall. The Park however, remains to the present day. John Rylands also founded the John Rylands Library recently amalgamated with the University of Manchester.

We will see how the cottage industries lived hand-in-hand with farming and how the old trades died out with the onset of the Industrial Revolution, forcing the workers back to the land as the market-gardening trade of Manchester increased. It is here that we see how the flooding of the area was overcome and the land reclaimed for farming.

The arrival of the Bridgewater Canal, which was the first artificial waterway in the country, in the mid-18th century, the opening of the railway in 1849 and the construction of the Manchester Ship Canal with its subsequent opening in 1894, all improved links to the rest of the country and to the sea, affecting the development of the area hugely. As transport and communications improved, jobs increased and the population numbers soared. This meant the necessary building of more housing of all types. The large villas that we see in Altrincham and Old Trafford also appeared in Stretford as the merchants of Manchester decided it was a pleasant place to live within travelling distance of the city. When Trafford Park was sold and developed into the huge Industrial Park that it eventually became, a workforce of thousands had to be accommodated. Houses were built in the vicinity and in the park itself, and entertainment and services provided.

Stretford has been the host for several major projects over the years. The Botanical Gardens, of 1831, provided a fashionable resort where people could spend their leisure time. The Art Exhibition, which was opened by Prince Albert and attended by Queen Victoria, was held there in 1857. The Stretford pageant, also a local tradition, has survived for years and photographs of this event also illustrate changing fashions.

Football was high on the agenda for the working man and was a popular Saturday afternoon's entertainment. The ground of one of the world's most famous clubs, Manchester United, is situated in Old Trafford.

Throughout its history, the area and the people of Stretford have been involved in several wars, including the Civil War and both World Wars. Stretford suffered badly during World War Two, most particularly because of its proximity to Trafford Park. Many of the companies there, including Metropolitan-Vickers, made a vital contribution to the war effort, manufacturing aircraft and aircraft components, making it an important target for the Germans. We show a map that demonstrates that the enemy had a clear knowledge of the layout of the park and the types of factories within it, so it is not surprising that Stretford suffered so badly from nightly air-raids.

RURAL STRETFORD

STRETFORD, as we know it today, is a large town located on the busy main route between Manchester and Chester. It is hard to imagine that the area was once a scattered rural area consisting of many acres of farmland, with beautiful views for many miles. Originally situated in the county of Lancashire, Stretford has since developed into an urban district. In the boundary changes of 1974, Stretford became part of the Metropolitan Borough of Trafford along with Sale, Altrincham and Urmston. Although many of the farms have long since gone, and the farmland has been replaced by housing, there are still some reminders of how the area looked, especially around Stretford Meadows, which is now part of the Mersey Valley.

Farming flourished and the early settlers to the area would have been attracted by the presence of a good soil base, which consisted mainly of loam and clay, and provided a suitable medium for growing crops, such as wheat,

Cob Hall Cottages were situated in the farmyard of Cob Hall Farm on Barton Road, at the junction of Sandy Lane. Today the area is occupied by Stretford House.

Gates Farm, Barton Road, was located on the corner of Sandy Lane. In 1881 it was inhabited by the Warburton family who farmed the 26 acres.

Old Trafford Toll Bar around the year 1869, looking along Chester Road. The toll bar was built around 1837, on what was thought to be the site of the old tithe barn. A charge was levied for anyone using the road, but there were some exclusions. These included members of the Royal Family, churchgoers, farmers transporting manure or farm goods, and clergymen who were visiting the sick.

Old Trafford Toll Bar, a view along Talbot Road in 1869.

The Pinfold or pound, pictured here in 1907, was used to hold stray animals. When livestock was transported on foot, occasionally some strayed. The owner had to pay a fine for their release.

barley and, later in the 20th century, rhubarb. Agriculture was to be the mainstay of the area and provided the inhabitants of Stretford with a reliable and convenient source of food as well as a continued source of income. The area also had a reliable water supply, being bordered by the River Mersey in the north and the River Irwell in the south, and would have been well-protected from any threat of attack by invaders. Being so close to the river, however, meant that flooding was problem, especially during the winter months. Throughout the centuries measures have had to be taken to combat the devastating effects of flooding. This included the building of

an overflow channel to control the level of water, and the construction of levies and sluices. During the latter part of the 20th century, the construction of Sale Water Park has also helped to address the problem of flooding, but there are still occasions, especially after heavy rainfall, when flooding occurs.

The names Crossford Bridge and Cross Street in the adjoining town of Sale, are a reminder of a time when flooding was a real problem. These names are thought to be associated with the wooden crosses which were used to mark a way through the road when the area was flooded.

Chester Road (Watling Street) links Chester to

Methodism was a strong force in Stretford during the 19th century and some of the first Independent Methodists in the area worshipped in a tent on land known as the Gravel. This soon proved inadequate as the congregation expanded quickly and larger premises had to be found. For some time they worshipped in an old barn on the corner of Toad Lane, close to Brunswick Street, before moving to a disused weaving shed. This was whitewashed and became known locally as the White Chapel until, 14 years later, the chapel in the photograph was built on land on Barton Road. In 1878 this building was declared unsafe and had to be demolished. The foundation stone for a new chapel was laid in 1879 and that chapel was finally opened in 1881.

These old buildings are thought to be those of Aurundal Farm, which was located on Barton Road.

Manchester and was originally constructed by the Romans during their occupation of Britain. Roman roads allowed for the quick movement of troops between their main garrison towns and usually followed a straight course, and Chester Road is no exception. Chester Road passes through Cheshire and crosses the old boundary with Lancashire at Crossford Bridge, continuing until it reaches the city of Manchester. The name of Stretford (Streetford) is thought to have derived from the Roman period, although there is little evidence to suggest that the Romans ever settled in the Stretford area. They were also thought to be the first to ford the River Mersey at the junction of Stretford and Sale, but the date of the first bridge is uncertain. We do know however that in 1533, John Leland, a commissioner for Henry VIII, wrote: 'I rode over Mersey water by a great bridge of tymber caulled Crosford Bridge.'

Early documents of Stretford record that there were originally two manors in the area – those of Stretford and Trafford. In the year 1212 Stretford, which was located close to Crossford Bridge, was held by Hamon de Mascy, for one ploughshare, while Trafford, which was closer to the River Irwell, was held by Henry de Trafford for a rent of 5s (25p) annually. Eventually the whole of Stretford passed to the de Trafford family and the two manors descended together. The area, which lay close to where the de Trafford family had their manor house, still retains its association with the that family and has become known as Old Trafford. The origin of the name of Old Trafford may be attributable to the time when there were two Trafford Halls. Local people, in order to

St Cuthbert's in Trafford Park was one of a number of churches built during the early 1900s to accommodate the residents of Trafford Park 'Village'. This photograph shows members of the congregation holding the banner that was carried during the Whit Walks of 1927–8.

distinguish between the two halls, named them Old Trafford Hall and New Trafford Hall. This was eventually abbreviated to Old Trafford, as the new hall, which became the residence of the de Trafford family, became known simply as Trafford Hall.

As the principle landowners, the de Trafford family leased out a large proportion of the land. Most of the tenants farmed at subsistence levels, while some of the larger farms were able to sell surplus produce at local markets. Some tenants worked from home in small cottage industries but there was no real heavy industry to speak of until the onset of the Industrial Revolution, and that was mostly focused on the city of Manchester and other areas of Lancashire. However, there was a papermill in 1765 and

some industry in the form of weaving, but on the whole the area was largely rural and relied heavily on farming. It was not until much later, during the early 1900s, that Trafford Park began to develop into an industrial area.

The early manorial records, parish records and those of the Stretford Court Baron are an invaluable source of information on early rural life. The Court Baron also gives us an insight into law and order. This was usually held on a rotational basis in one of the public houses – the Trafford Arms, the Old Cock Inn, the Dog and Partridge are all mentioned along with others. The Court Baron was a manorial court and was held to sort out estate matters and to deal with misdemeanors such as 'getting turf for fuel' or allowing cattle to graze on common land after

Edge Lane Methodist Chapel
was built in 1862. It was built
from stone in the Gothic style.
The church was designed by a
Mr Fuller of London, cost
£13,000 and provided seating
for up to 500 people. The
steeple was a local landmark
and could be seen for many
miles. It was demolished in the
1960s to allow for the
widening of Edge Lane.

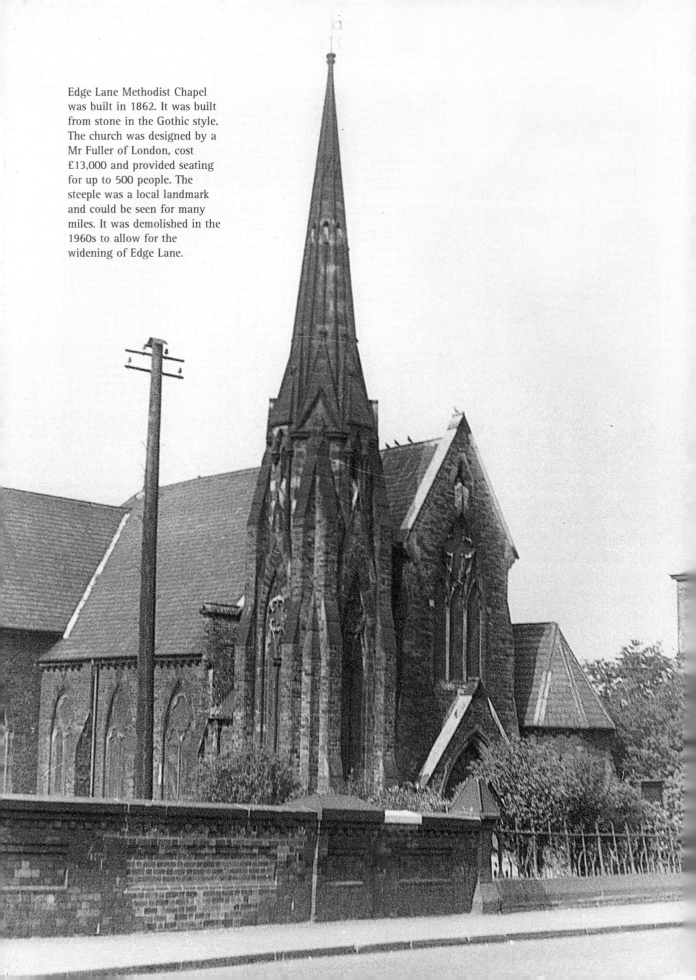

This farm building was situated on Barton Road and indicates how Stretford must have looked in times gone by. The lane on the left gives a brief view of how rural the landscape appeared.

set dates. These offences are referred to frequently and were punished by fines. It was important, in a small community, that tenants adhered to the strict rules of local government. Despite this, offences were many, for example:

> 1701: 'Margaret, wife of James Deane, and Elizabeth, wife of James Sidebotham, for hedge breaking – fine 6 shillings.'

> 1706: 29 persons fined for not ditching and slaucing [draining] their parts on Lostock Moss, Longford Moss and Edge Moss, and nine persons, including Mr Trafford, for not ditching and slaucing their parts of Longford brook.'

In 1666 it was recorded that there were 117 hearths taxed, of which Cecil de Trafford held 24. The hearth tax was levied on houses which were above 20 shillings in value, and is a good indication as to the wealth of a particular area. Throughout its history Stretford remained in the background of daily life in England and did not feature in any major events until the Jacobite rebellion of 1745 when Bonnie Prince Charlie advanced on London from the north, although, of course, he got only as far as Derby before turning back. Crossford Bridge was situated in a strategic position on the River Mersey and, as there was no other access point for many miles either side, the bridge was destroyed by the Liverpool Blues. It was quickly rebuilt, however, as it was situated in such a key position.

As we have mentioned, much of everyday rural life was based around farming; this

As Stretford gradually lost land given over to housing, Mitford Street was an example of how things were changing. By 1898 the Ordnance Survey map and other records indicate that the road was made up of terraced housing. However, some of the original thatched cottages still remained, as can be seen from this photograph which was taken around that time.

included livestock as well as crops. Pigs were farmed as a source of food and also for resale, often being the main source of income when they were sold in the Manchester markets. They are constantly referred to in many of the early records and, during the 18th and 19th centuries, controlling them appeared to have been a persistent problem. Complaints were many and in 1794 a notice was posted on the chapel door 'that if any person suffers pigs to ramble about, he will have to pay five shillings for each offence'. However, it wasn't just wandering pigs that bothered people. In 1778–80, the Revd Mr Clarke complained to the magistrates about the pork butchers 'who were selling leftover meat in the market on a Sabbath'.

Law and order was the responsibility of the parish constables, who were also responsible for ensuring that the stocks and places of imprisonment were maintained. The stocks were situated somewhere in the vicinity of the junction of King Street and Chester Road, but the exact location is not known. It seems that the safety of people and property also fell under the remit of the constables who, in 1782, ordered 'that no person shall carry any fire from thatched house to thatched house uncovered lest a spark should be blown on to the thatch and cause a conflagration'.

At a meeting held at the Angel Inn on 12 March 1862, the constables were named as: S.W. Greaves, Edward Cleaver and Charles Taylor, all of Edge Lane, Charles Timperley of Lostock Hall, James Ackerley of Hullard Hall and John Taylor of Waters Meeting.

From the 19th century more records, such as

This farm was situated on the corner of Derbyshire Lane and Pinnington Lane and was known locally as Jimmy Bear's and Billy Benn's.

The Independent Methodist Church on Barton Road was built to replace the previous one which had to be demolished in 1878, due to its unsafe condition. Material from the old church was reused in the new chapel and members of the congregation worked evenings and weekends to help with the construction. The chapel took three years to complete, during which time the congregation worshipped in temporary accommodation on land off Urmston Lane. It was finally opened in 1881. The organ was donated by Sir Thomas Robinson and remained in use for over 75 years. In 1902, a row of five houses were pulled down and the vacant land was used to build a Sunday school, which opened in 1903.

This cottage stood on Moss Road. After its demolition, Mr John Maunders used the vacant land to build a cinema for his daughter. The cinema was named the Corona and remained open until Metropolitan-Vickers bought it in 1951.

Ordnance Survey maps, the official census and street directories, become available for research, and the information they provide helps us to understand how the town of Stretford has developed. *Pigot's Directory* for 1836 lists the following information for 'Pubs and Trades':

Esther Aldred, victualler, the Wheatsheaf

Hannah Hale, victualler, the Robin Hood

Elizabeth Hazlehurst, victualler, the Old Cock

James Hulme, victualler, the Bull and Punch Bowl

John Kent, victualler, the Bishop Blaize

Thomas Tattersall, victualler, the Dog and Partridge

Samuel Watson, victualler, the Angel Inn

Joseph Dean, blacksmith

Thomas M. Fisher, cotton manufacturer and brickmaker

John Gibbon, pork butcher

James Wigglesworth, pork butcher

John Taylor, pork butcher

James Shawcross, pork butcher

Joseph Rogerson, pork butcher

Thomas Raingill, pork butcher

Hannah Pixton, pork butcher

Peter Morris, pork butcher

James Lowe, pork butcher

As the list shows, the area relied heavily on the butchering of pigs as a source of income and, during the 1830s, around 800 to 1,000 pigs were slaughtered weekly. The pigs were brought

Ivy Farm, which was situated at the corner of Highfield Road and Chester Road.

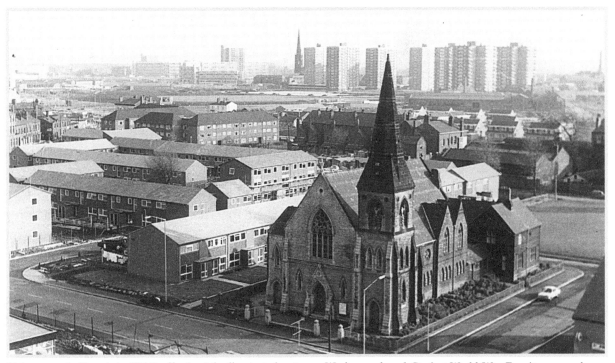

St Lawrence's Church in Old Trafford originally started out as a Wesleyan chapel. During World War Two it was used as a mortuary and, later, as a warehouse, before finally being taken over by the Catholic church.

Crossford Bridge Toll Bar was one of the Stretford booths where users had to pay the necessary toll to use the road. In 1750 an Act of Parliament had been passed for the turnpiking of Crossford Bridge and this Act continued to be in force until 1 November 1872.

in from surrounding areas, as well as from Ireland and Wales. After being driven through the streets of Stretford to the butchers they were then slaughtered. The pork which was produced was then sold on Manchester's markets. Stretford became known locally as 'Porkhampton' or 'Black Pudding Junction' and the locals earned the nickname the 'Stretford Black Puddings'. The area was renowned for its black puddings, which were a by-product from the butchering. A local dish was known as Stretford Goose and consisted of pork stuffed with sage and onions. It was said that local people would move the furniture out of their houses to make room for the hams to hang while they were being cured or salted. This often took around three months before the meat was ready for eating. The major crop grown in the area was rhubarb, which was often referred to as 'Stretford beef'.

Until the 19th century most of the housing development had taken place along both sides of the main Stretford Road. It is noticeable, however, that the town had developed in two sections (Ordnance Survey, 1848). One section was centered on St Matthew's Church (built 1842), close to the border with Sale, while the other area was around Old Trafford. The

The church of St Matthew was built to replace an earlier church, which had originally been erected during the reign of Elizabeth I and was rebuilt sometime around 1714. This earlier church was demolished in 1841, and in October 1842 the Bishop of Chester consecrated the new church of St Matthew's. St Matthew's was built from brick and stone and was enlarged in 1861 to seat 1,070 people. The earliest parish registers date from 1592. The original burial ground for the inhabitants of Stretford was also here and one of the earliest references is for the burial of Elizabeth, wife of John Bent, who died on 2 January 1683.

development in the Old Trafford area was close to Trafford Hall, the residence of the de Trafford family. Despite these small pockets of occupation, Stretford was still largely rural, traversed only by small country lanes and footpaths. Today it is hard to imagine that on the corner of the busy junction of Sandy Lane and Barton Road, there was once a single cottage (Oak Cottage), which was surrounded by open views for many miles.

The roads, which were often little more than tracks, were dry and dusty in the summer and muddy during the winter when, on occasion, they became impassable. Some major roads were known as turnpike roads and these were owned and maintained by turnpike trusts. Users had to pay a small toll and the toll collection points were called 'Bars'. Two such points were Trafford Bar and Brooks Bar, names still in use today, although many people are unaware of their history. There was also a toll bar at Mersey Bridge. Trafford Toll Bar, which was built around 1837, was on the site of an ancient tithe barn. The charge for a one-horse vehicle was 9d, but this was reduced to 6d in 1842 to encourage more people to use it.

With the opening of the railway on 21 July 1849, transport links became easier, and people began to travel further afield. Stations were built at Old Trafford and Stretford and the railway

The bells of St Matthew's are seen here, having been taken down for repair. They were sent to the foundry of John Taylor in Loughborough. St Matthew's Church originally had only one bell but this had been increased to six in 1870, when Mr Henry Hayes of Edge Lane donated another five in memory of his late wife. The six bells were first rung on St Thomas's Day, 1870. In 1933 two more bells were added to make a total of eight.

now provided an additional form of transport to that offered by the roads, and the packet boats travelling on the Bridgewater Canal. Many people, though, still walked everywhere, or, if they were lucky enough to afford it, would travel by horse and cart. The omnibus ran hourly from Altrincham to Manchester and although the journey was slow, at least it was less hard work than walking. The fare from Manchester to Stretford was 1s 0d if you sat inside, reduced to 9d if you braved the weather and sat outside. The Angel Inn was a stopover point and provided a comfortable area for waiting.

The church played a large role in rural life in Stretford, as it did everywhere in England. Prior to the building of the first church in Stretford, locals had to travel four miles into Manchester, usually on foot, to worship. The date of the earliest chapel is not known, but is mentioned in 1577 (Saxton's map of Lancashire) and in 1717 a public meeting was held to rebuild the chapel on the corner of Chapel Lane. The cost was £500, which is around £50,000 in today's relative value. The rebuilding included galleries and a partition where the more wealthy families would sit. In September 1841, Lady de Trafford laid the foundation stone for the church of St Matthew's on an area known as Wagstaffe field. The church cost a total of £2,700 and was designed by William Hayley. It was consecrated on 10 October 1842. Stretford had an abundance of

The bell ringers of St Matthew's seen in this photograph were also very proficient at handbell ringing. The handbells can be seen neatly laid out on the grass.

churches: All Saints' Church situated on the corner of School Road and Cyprus Street was built in 1884–5; St Thomas's was consecrated 1857; St Bride's (1877–8); St Hilda's was completed in 1900 but damaged by bombs in the blitz of 1940, the new building situated on Warwick Road South being opened in 1965. Others include St Cuthbert's (1902); St John's (1908); St Peter's (1916). Catholic churches included, St Anne's (1863), St Antony's (1904), St Alphonsus (1909), St Hugh of Lincoln, St Teresa's, St Lawrence's. There were also many Non-conformist churches, which had started to spring up around the country as other forms of worship became more popular. The Independent Methodist Church, which originally met in a tent, was set up on land known as 'the Gravel' in King Street. Other churches were the City Road Wesleyan Church, the Methodist Church, the Primitive Methodist Church, the Congregational Church, the Union Baptist, the Sharon Church, the Christadelphian Church, the Martin Luther Kirche and the Plymouth Brethren Church. Many of the churches were built around the early part of the 20th century, at a time when the population of Stretford was on the increase.

As the 19th century wore on, Stretford became a desirable place to live. Situated close to the border of Manchester, it had become a fashionable area. The Botanical Gardens, built in 1831, consisted of 17 acres and provided a lovely venue for a stroll or an afternoon out. Large grand houses were constructed to provide homes for the city businessmen, especially in the area around Trafford Lane, and, very gradually, the rural landscape began to change.

Throstle Nest in 1923. Both these views, dated 1923 and 1951 respectively, show the area after industrialisation. It is hard to imagine that the area was once a local beauty spot, well-known for the songs of the thrushes, or throstles as they were known locally, which is where the name is thought to have originated. Throstle Nest was located approximately in the Cornbrook area, close to where the old paperworks stood. Although well-known for its beauty, it was also infamous as a place where highwaymen would lay in wait to rob unfortunate travellers who were passing through.

The first Congregational Church was built on Chorlton Street in 1861, using part of the proceeds raised from the sale of a chapel on Cannon Street. At a later date another chapel was built on Chester Road, opposite Market Street, and this was eventually replaced by a larger stone building, which included a Sunday school.

This photograph of Beech Farm was taken from Stretford House in 1971. At one time the farm was owned and run by Mr John Brundritt, who also held interests in the local bus service which ran from Stretford to Manchester. The farmland stretched over a wide area, with some as far as Stretford Moss.

Valentine's Farm on Poplar Road, pictured in 1882. At one time it was known locally as Bradshaw's Nursery.

This orchard was situated behind Valentine's Farm. The group of people in the photograph are thought to be members of the Valentine family.

Many farms were known by the name of the farmer, rather than possessing a name of their own. This one had been known as Hancock's Farm, but at the time of this photograph it was called Bradshaw's Farm after Mr Samuel Bradshaw who was a tenant farmer. At one time Samuel Bradshaw also farmed Porch House Farm. The farmhouse stood opposite the site of the present Robin Hood Hotel.

Longford Bridge Farm, pictured here in 1938, was at one time numbered 1001 and 1003 Chester Road. The land spanned both sides of Chester Road. During its history it was also known as Hancock's Farm and Nicholson's Farm.

It was Esther Cookson who founded the first Primitive Methodist Church in Stretford, in 1829. Mr Frances Gibbon was so impressed by the work of the church that he offered a barn for church services. In 1877 the foundation stone for a new church was laid, which included a time capsule containing documents related to the church. After the church was completed there was still a large debt of £4,000 outstanding. Members of the congregation worked very hard to reduce this and prepared a grand bazaar to raise money. An archway was built at the entrance gates and flags decorated King Street. The bazaar was a great success and managed to raise £500. Efforts to raise money continued but it wasn't until 1907 that the debt was finally cleared.

St Anne's Roman Catholic Church was built in 1863, on land that was donated by Sir Humphrey de Trafford. The final cost amounted to £24,000. It was designed by the famous Victorian architect Augustus Pugin, whose work included Birmingham Cathedral and St Mary's Roman Catholic Church in Derby. St Anne's was consecrated by Bishop Turner in 1867 and in the following year the organ was installed. The angelus bell was erected in 1899; it weighed over one ton and was transported all the way from Ireland. The stonework found near the entrance contains tributes to Sir Humphrey and Lady Annette de Trafford.

Wellington Farm stood behind St Matthew's Church and was possibly named to celebrate the famous victory of Wellington at the Battle of Waterloo in 1815. The farm was built some time during the 19th century, but the exact date is not known. It was the home of the Derbyshire family and the location of their family haulage business. It was demolished in 1966 to make way for the redevelopment of Stretford town centre.

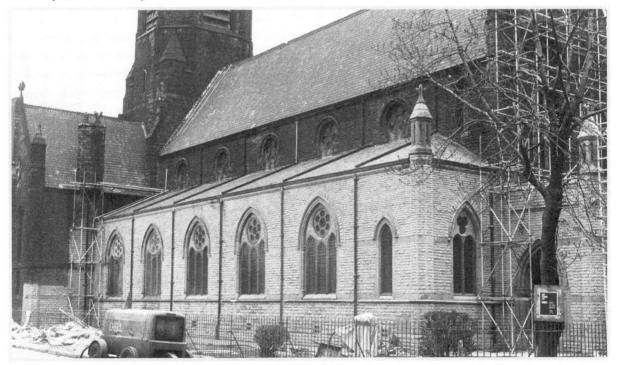

St Bride's Church began as small mission built on a cricket field in Cornbrook Street in 1863. The Shrewsbury church was built in 1877–8 at cost of £7,000, but the addition of a chancel, apse, transepts and spire, together with a rectory, added a further £3,000. The photograph shows the church undergoing cleaning in April 1973 as part of a special environment assistance scheme.

White House Farm, Gorse Hill, stood opposite the Trafford Hotel facing Chester Road. It was demolished in the 1930s.

Sexton Bradshaw, whose role was that of a paid church official. Responsibilities included grave-digging, bell-ringing, cleaning the church and opening the pews.

Manor House was situated on Poplar Road. This photograph was taken around 1938.

Boundary Farm was situated on the old boundary of Stretford and included a farmhouse and 12 acres of farmland. The 1881 census recorded that the farm was occupied by the Kelsall family which consisted of John Kelsall, aged 52, his wife Elizabeth, aged 34, their sons John, 25, and Charles, nine, and one daughter Alice, aged three months. Presumably John was Elizabeth's stepson.

New Shed Farm, seen here in 1963, was situated at the corner of Barton Road and Sandy Lane and during one period also went under the name of Mellor's Farm. In 1881 New Shed Farm was made up of 81 acres. The farm was occupied by the Bancroft family, which consisted of William Bancroft, aged 29, his wife Mary, 23, and two sons, William, two, and Joseph, eight months.

Porch House Farm on Chester Road was at one time the Pack Horse Inn. It stood on the same side of the road as the Angel Hotel, close to the corner of Green Street. The building dates from around 1714.

Turn Moss Farm, showing the rear of the building. The pump of the shallow well can be seen to the left of the outhouse.

The fields around Turn Moss date from around the time of the last Ice Age, when mossland covered large areas of the landscape. Many mossland areas have been since been drained and built on, but some, such as Hale Moss and Turn Moss in Stretford, have been left relatively untouched.

INDUSTRY AND COMMERCE

I
T IS thought that as early as 1540, the wool trade had an impact on Stretford. Flixton, its neighbour, was at one time called Fleecetown which suggests an occupation to do with the wool trade, and the public house in Stretford facing Edge Lane was called the Bishop Blaize. It was said that a bishop of that name was the patron saint of woolcombers, and as sheep were plentiful around Stretford at that time, a conclusion could be drawn that locals did indeed follow this trade.

As Stretford was situated on the main road from Chester to Manchester, many people passed through it on their travels. The earliest form of

Waters Meeting on the Bridgewater Canal, so called because this is the junction of the sections of the canal that go to Manchester, Leigh and the Preston Brook junction. This photograph shows 150 Moss Road on the right bank and numbers 152–154 on the left bank.

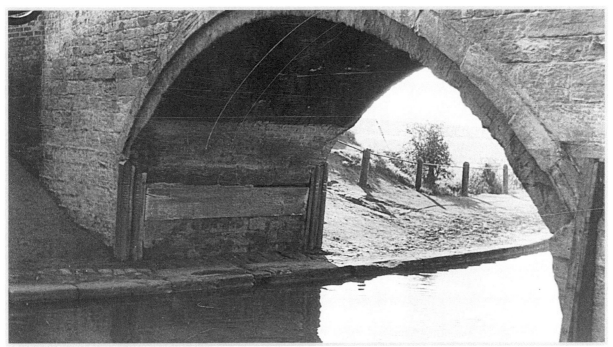

Taylor's Bridge on Moss Road was originally built over the Bridgewater Canal to provide access to the Trafford Park land. It was almost hump-backed and only one vehicle at a time could pass over it. When the de Traffords sold Trafford Park and Westinghouse works was built, Moss Road became an important route into the park for their employees, so the old bridge was widened. It was also known as Joshua's Bridge or Joshua Taylor's Bridge. There was a Joshua Taylor, a chapel warden in 1769, who lived in a farmhouse which was demolished in 1855, near Waters Meeting. It is possible the bridge was named after him.

The watch house, shown here c.1906, near Cut Hole Bridge on the Bridgewater Canal. This was the canal maintenance staff house and there was usually a boat moored to the bank, containing materials for repairing the canal. The occupants of the watch house would shore up the sides of the canal when flooding threatened the bridge. Barfoot, Barfoothough or Barfooty Bridge, as it was known locally, carries the Bridgewater Canal over Stretford Ees, which are the low-lying meadows between Stretford and Sale. It is said that it took 2,000 oak piles driven into the earth to strengthen the bridge (*S. James's Chronicle*, 1765). It looks as though the man on the roof is giving the wall a coat of whitewash. The sign on the wall is an advertisement for MacDonald's Teeth. There was a dentist called MacDonald's on Edge Lane, who patented ceramic teeth.

The Earl of Ellesmere's state barge on the Bridgewater Canal. The barge looks very full and the occupants seem to be enjoying themselves.

transport through Stretford was by packhorse or stagecoach, and the inns and hostelries grew up partly because of this traffic. The Angel Inn and the Trafford Arms were their main stopping places. We also see trades such as blacksmiths, wheelwrights and saddlers developing. The last stagecoach through Stretford is thought to have been in the 1840s.

The Bridgewater Canal was also a means of transporting both goods and people to and from Manchester. It was built by the Duke of Bridgewater together with James Brindley and was the first man made waterway of its kind. The duke had coal interests in Worsley and wanted to find a better way of transporting that coal. The Stretford to Manchester stretch of the canal was opened in 1761 and ran from Worsley

to Stretford and to Manchester. The building of this stretch necessitated the construction of the aqueduct over the River Irwell at Barton. This aqueduct was hailed as a great feat of engineering and was visited by many. The Bridgewater extension, which started at Longford Bridge and passed through Stretford and Sale, was opened in 1795. In 1907 a packet boat service was started. The boats were drawn by horses with riders and collected passengers from Stretford taking them to Ducks Dock and Knott Mill. Industries grew along the canal and boatyards began to open up. One of the first was Henry Rathbone & Son, who had a yard on Edge Lane on the canal bank. Another member of this family built a yard near Longford Bridge. Inman's Rustic Works were on the canal side

An unpowered barge takes people on an outing on the Bridgewater Canal *c.*1890. Notice the rope at the front of the boat by which it is being towed.

Inside Rathbone's boatyard, which was the oldest of the three boatyards in Stretford which built canal barges. Some of these barges can be seen moored on the canal at the rear of the photograph.

Woodcutters stop to pose for the cameraman in Poole's Yard in the later years of the 19th century.

next to the boat yard. The 1898 *Directory of Stretford* lists the Bridgewater Trustees, Fred Hulme, Albert Coleman and the Wigan Coal and Iron Company, as coal merchants on Edge Lane, and Fellows, Morton & Clayton Ltd as carriers and boat builders.

Up until the 1820s, one of the most important industries in Stretford was the hand weaving of cotton. The area had long been associated with cotton production, since the damp climate had been essential for the spinning process. There were 302 looms in the village and 780 souls involved in the cotton industry. However, by 1826 only four of those looms were in use, as the effects of the Industrial Revolution of the late 17th and early 18th centuries had filtered down to rural areas. In 1779 there were riots in Manchester as machinery replaced the old hand looms and, sure enough, the machines eventually took away the trade of the home weavers in Stretford. Times were hard and the people of Stretford had to think of other ways to make a living. The soil was fertile and Manchester had an excellent market, so agriculture was the natural choice of most, in particular the cultivation of rhubarb. Land was let in strips and local folk worked hard to make ends meet. The pig industry continued to flourish. Large sheds, each holding up to 1,500 pigs, were erected to contain the animals. Every part of the pig was used when it was slaughtered. It is said that enough money was made out of the sale of the bristles to build a row of houses called, aptly, Bristle Row.

The railway opened in Stretford in 1849, the first station master being Mr W.H. Bowers and the first porter Thomas Massey. There was a bus service from Flixton to Stretford Station, run by John Greenwood, the fare being 6d outside (on top) and 8d inside the bus. Mr John Swarbrick was the first station master at Old Trafford. There was now an easier link to Manchester and the population of Stretford grew, as people who worked in the city decided to live in the more rural areas. The knock-on effect of increased population was an improvement in services and commerce. Shops such as bootmakers, tailors, butchers and grocers sprung up in the village. In the *Directory of Stretford* for 1898 there is listed a laundry, milliner and tobacconist. In fact most things that were required could be found in the village. More public houses appeared and, in 1898, the landlord of the Old Cock was William Mann.

It was decided, in 1852, that Stretford should have the benefit of gas lighting. A meeting was held in the Trafford Arms on 7 January to discuss the matter, and subsequently a plot of land sited near Longford Bridge, where Foster's Farm stood, was purchased and a gasworks built on it. The Stretford Gas Company was established with a capital of £2,861 10s and it was to supply gas to Stretford and the surrounding areas. The first chairman was Joseph Brundrett.

Lewis's coach's in 1892. This coach ran between Manchester and Liverpool. The enterprising Frank Hulme took photographs of the passengers early in the morning and had prints ready to sell on the evening of the return trip.

*Venu*s, the first railway engine to pass through Stretford, on 21 July 1849. In 1847 it had been decided that a railway line should connect Manchester and Altrincham. Thus the Manchester South Junction & Altrincham Railway provided Stretford with two stations, one in the village and one at Old Trafford. The Parliamentary Bill to allow it was opposed by Lord Ellesmere, who claimed that the railway would interfere with passenger and goods traffic on the Bridgewater Canal. Eventually he agreed to give up his passenger service and the railway went ahead.

Tramcar on Barton Road, Stretford. In 1845 Stretford was introduced to public transport in the form of the two-horse tramcar. Massey's tramcars left the Unicorn Inn in Altrincham for Manchester every hour. The drop-off point in Stretford was the Angel Hotel. This tramcar belongs to the Manchester Carriage & Tramcar Company which operated between Manchester and Old Trafford.

The site of electricity works in Stretford. The lighting order for the area was obtained in 1897 and the electricity station was erected next to Longford Bridge. The charge for private lighting was 6d per unit. The area that was supplied later included Flixton, Urmston and Davyhulme.

In 1856 the company was registered under the Joint Stock Companies Act. In 1862 an Act of Incorporation was obtained, which was necessary to protect the company's owners as they were to dig up the public highway to lay mains.

In 1765, on the site of what was thought to have once been a corn mill belonging to Trafford Manor, there was a papermill. It stood on land near Throstle Nest, which was leased partly from the Irwell Navigation Company and partly from the Trafford Estate. The *Manchester Mercury* ran an article on the 20 March 1721 advertising for sale the 'newly-erected Paper Mill, for the making of writing and printing paper, with engines, dwelling houses, stables and an acre and a half of land situated in Stretford near the Duke of Bridgewater Canal, on the banks of the navigable Irwell where vessels are daily passing and repassing.' In 1818 the papermill burnt down. It was rebuilt but the property was eventually bought and demolished by the Manchester Ship Canal Company.

The most important events in the history of Stretford, as a commercially viable area, were the building of the Manchester Ship Canal and the subsequent sale of Trafford Park by Sir Humphrey de Trafford. These two events changed the landscape and impacted on the lives of the people living in Stretford and the surrounding townships, to a large degree changing what had formerly been a rural area to a busy thriving community. The ship canal opened in 1894, at last giving Manchester access to the sea.

The then owners of Trafford Park, the de Trafford family, initially objected to the construction of the ship canal, which would run through their land. By way of compensation for the land they would lose, the Manchester Ship Canal Company gave the de Traffords additional land to the north, as well as two wharves for their personal use. Of course, although men came from all over the country to work on the massive project, the building of the canal brought employment to the area itself.

Trafford Park was sold soon after the opening of the Manchester Ship Canal. The development of the park made it the largest industrial estate in Europe at the time, and determined the sweeping changes that took place in Stretford. Although the park was, at first, opened to the public, companies soon began to move in. The Manchester Fuel and Patent Company was one of the first to open, in 1898, followed by Morrison Ingram who were sanitary engineers, and Bennett's saw mills. A railway system was installed, as the area was so large, and bigger companies started to take up land. W.T. Glover & Co, a cable manufacturer from Salford, had completely relocated to Trafford Park by 1902 and agreed to supply electricity to the estate. The arrival of Westinghouse, an American company who realised the great potential of Trafford Park as a UK base prompted the build-

Stretford gas works in 1947. Notice the tennis court and the Bridgewater Canal in the distance. Westinghouse Works were directly behind the gas works in Trafford Park, so it is likely that the industry seen in the far distance is that area.

HOT WATER!

By Jingo! those 'Ascot' people were right

'Ascot' Water Heaters supply hot water to all taps, and at any time of the day. Will work separately or with your present system.

per **7/6** quarter
fixed and maintained free.

STRETFORD & DISTRICT GAS BOARD
Telephone LONgford 1133

Advertisement for the Stretford & District Gas Board, from a 1936 Stretford pageant programme.

ing of the new houses within the park's perimeters. These houses were built in a rectangular pattern much in the style of American towns, having numbered streets and avenues. The 'Village', as it came to be known, had its own school, church and shops. In 1907 the population was 3,060. In the 1927 *Directory of Manchester,* the estate is listed as a separate community. Miss Henrietta Fletcher CMB is a midwife living on Second Avenue. There is a plumber on Fifth Street, and S. Hall Jnr, a constable, also resides there, at number 116. Confectioners, butchers, tobacconists, newsagents and grocers all make a living in the Village and it even has its own doctor, Mr Ian Ernest Hutton White MD who was also a

surgeon, with his surgery at Fairview on Fourth Avenue. It would seem the community was quite self-sufficient.

The development of Trafford Park changed Stretford in many ways. The population grew rapidly as promises of work drew people to the area. In 1881 the population of Stretford was 1,477, in 1901 it was 30,436 and by 1921 numbered 46,535. Housing and amenities were built to accommodate this boom and to support a different way of life. The land that had previously been covered by farms and market gardens was now sold and built on, and so the occupations of the residents turned from that of the land to supporting growing nearby industries. However, the park began to decline in the 1960s as manufacturing products decreased, and business suffered until a rejuvenation programme was commenced in the 1980s. The type of business in Trafford Park became predominantly that of warehousing and distribution. The Trafford Park Estate Company offered lower rents to encourage new firms and the Civic Trust for the North-West landscaped neglected areas and planted trees to make the park more attractive for its workforce. Gone are the days of big industry and pollution and the park is a much more pleasant place to work. It has survived decades of change and hopefully will continue to prosper.

As the occupations of individuals in the Village in Trafford Park reflected the needs of the people living and working there, so did those of the people of Stretford. Every community needs work, leisure facilities, social care and commercial enterprises such as shops to enable people to spend their well-earned money. As industry thrived in the area and people became wealthier, shops began to diversify. Cinemas

Throstle Nest weir and lock. In the foreground are the excavations for Salford Docks, part of the Manchester Ship Canal complex. In the background are the ruins of the papermill.

were built and new public houses appeared. As this growth continued in the 1950s and 1960s, the centre of Stretford, which included King Street where the majority of shops lay, became very congested and it was decided that a shopping precinct should be built.

King Street shops were demolished together with the houses on that stretch, the residents

Facing work at Mode Wheel Locks during the building of the Manchester Ship Canal. Mode Wheel was situated in the most important section of the Manchester Ship Canal, that being the Barton-Manchester section. Some 2,800 men worked on this section alone, together with 26 horses, 30 locomotives, seven steam-navvies, three cranes and seven french excavators (an excavator with a bucket on a conveyor belt). The locks, together with a weir, however, were in existence before the canal was built. They were put in place by the old Navigation Company on the River Irwell and had an extensive group of flour and logwood mills attached to them, which used the river fall for power. There was a foreign animals wharf projected at Mode Wheel with pens for the cattle, a huge market and an abattoir. There were also oil tanks erected there, the first tanker unloading its cargo from America on 24 July 1897.

Queen Victoria's yacht *Enchantress* leaving for Mode Wheel Locks. The Queen performed the opening ceremony of the Manchester Ship Canal on 21 May 1894. This was done by pressing a button, which opened the gates of Mode Wheel Locks. Queen Victoria also knighted the Mayor of Manchester and the Mayor of Salford whilst aboard the *Enchantress*.

being housed in newly-built Stretford House, a tall block of flats erected close to where the shopping centre would be. The first stage of the development was finished in 1969 and the second phase in 1974. The precinct has its advantages – it is under cover and traffic free. However, many feel that the heart has been torn out of Stretford and that the building is unattractive from the outside. Most of the old shops were lost, as were the swimming baths and the Trafford Arms.

Stretford Precinct now lies under the threat of the Trafford Centre which represents the latest trends in leisure and retail business. The theme of the Stretford centre has been quite carefully based on Trafford and if one looks closely enough, some of the historical figures of the area can be seen gazing down on the busy scene.

Trafford Road decorative arch built for the opening of number-nine dock on the Manchester Ship Canal. Edward VII performed the ceremony on 13 July 1905. The dock was constructed between 1902 and 1905, on the site of the former racecourse.

Trafford Park entrance on Trafford Park Road.

Mixture of countryside and industry early in the early 1900s, on the site of Westinghouse & Co.

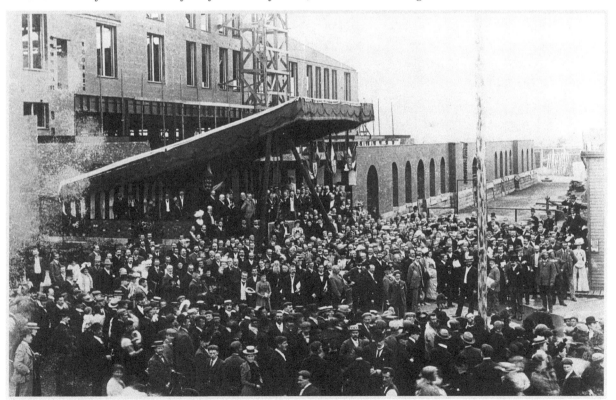

The laying of the foundation stone of Westinghouse on 3 August 1901. Coins of the realm were placed under the stone, which was laid jointly by the Lord Mayors of London and Manchester. Building started in June that year and the whole project was completed in in under 12 months. The company's premises were sometimes known as the Big House.

George Westinghouse (seated left) and some of the early directors of the company.

James Stewart & Co, surveyors, who came from America to survey the site for Westinghouse & Co.

The pattern shop at Westinghouse on 7 May 1902.

Interior of the Ford Motor Company's premises on Third Avenue. The company opened at Trafford Park on 23 October 1911, after being established in the UK in March of that year. The British Electric Car Company on Westinghouse Road had formerly used the site.

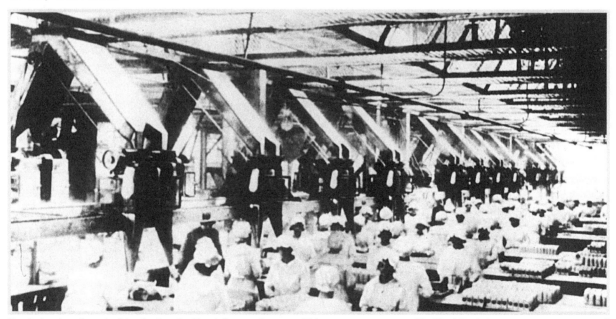

Tea being hand-packed in the Brooke Bond factory in 1930. This company came to Trafford Park in 1918 to occupy one of the hives. Nineteen of these hives were contained in one long building on Mosley Road, each measuring 25ft wide with road access to the front and railway access to the rear. The low rent of £80 per annum encouraged companies who later often built larger permanent premises, as did Brooke Bond four years later.

The Bishop Blaize, Chester Road, was situated near to the old cross facing Edge Lane. It was a thatched, whitewashed building with stone floors and with stables on one side. It was demolished in 1863 and the Talbot Hotel was built on the site.

The Wheatsheaf Inn was located on Chester Road, on the corner of Market Street. It was also known as Bowker's, as that was the name of the landlord at one time. The name is shown on this photograph. Mr Bowker was said to weigh 25st. Next to the inn stands a boot and shoemakers, W. Coventry.

The construction of Carborundum Co Ltd in June 1913. Note Trafford Park Lake on the far right.

The Talbot Hotel on
Chester Road was
probably named after
Mary Annette Talbot,
who married of Sir
Humphrey de Trafford
in 1855.

The Trafford Arms stood on the corner of King Street and
Chester Road and was next to the Cross, where four roads
met. It was a stopping-off place for travellers and the base
stone of the demolished cross, which lay next to the inn, was
used by riders to mount their horses. In 1777 it was known
as the Bull's Head. At one time the inn brewed its own beer,
and it was also the headquarters for pig dealers and featured
a large pig pen.

Francis Worrall, the last landlord of the Trafford Arms.

The Bridge Inn near Crossford Bridge, Chester Road, showing both the old building and the new. The inn was on the Cheshire side of the river but was still within Lancashire. It was often flooded since the entrance was reached by a set of steps below street level.

The Old Cock in 1870 showing the horse omnibus terminus on the Crossford Bridge side of the inn, Again, this hostelry brewed its own beer at one time and it was a calling place for carters on their way to Manchester with produce. There were stables next to it, which were later turned into a wheelwright's workshop, and it was the terminus for the Manchester Carriage Company.

This photograph was taken from the side of the Old Cock Inn, showing the corner of Barton Road and Chester Road.

The Angel Inn stood opposite the parish church, and this photograph shows the Angel on the left with the houses next to the church on the right. The inn was used as a setting-down and picking-up point for the early stage coaches, and later trams and buses. It had a fine bowling green at the rear. Bosdin Leech describes it as an old-fashioned building with small whitewashed windows, and of it being very cosy with good food. There was, at one time, a tall pump facing the building to draw water for use at the inn. Important property sales in the district were held at the Angel.

The Robin Hood Inn, which used to be called the Wagon and Horses, stood at the corner of King Street and Higgin Lane (later Barton Road). The old building was demolished in 1882.

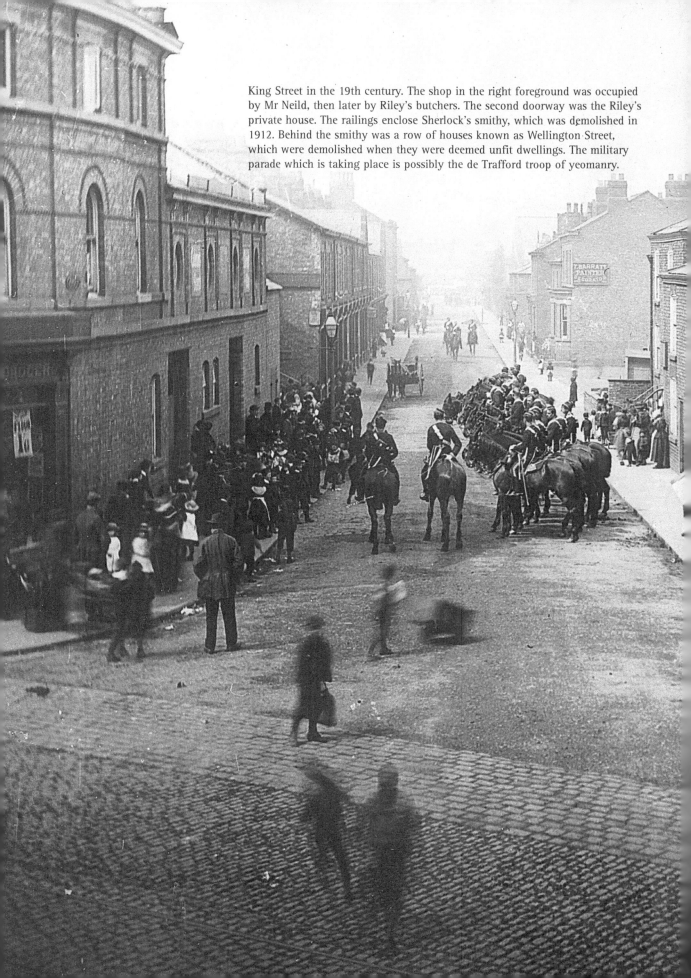

King Street in the 19th century. The shop in the right foreground was occupied by Mr Neild, then later by Riley's butchers. The second doorway was the Riley's private house. The railings enclose Sherlock's smithy, which was demolished in 1912. Behind the smithy was a row of houses known as Wellington Street, which were demolished when they were deemed unfit dwellings. The military parade which is taking place is possibly the de Trafford troop of yeomanry.

Jimmy Benn's store on Pennington Lane (later Victoria Road) about 1898.

Broadbent's chemist shop at 1177 Chester Road, between Harrop & Son, tailors, and Burston and Nixson, greengrocers.

This is Harrop the tailors' old shop at 97 Chester Road. We can see the first few letters of the next shop, which is probably Brereton's chemist and druggist, who are listed in the 1948 *Directory of Stretford* as trading on Chester Road. In later years the shop was numbered 1177 Chester Road.

Seymour Mead & Co, 1171 Chester Road, on the corner of Newton Street. In the window are advertisements for pork sausages, priced 7d and 8d per lb, and Wiltshire bacon. The corner window has a display of coffee and on the left there are advertisements for 'spring cleaning requisites'. The extreme right-hand window has a display of tinned pears and advertisements for Hall's Wine, which apparently cured influenza.

Mr J.W. Moss poses outside his Supper Bar on King Street c.1908.

Wakefield's shop at the corner of King Street and Chester Road. This building was on the site of the Trafford Arms and survived until the transformation of Stretford when the Arndale Centre was built. It was known as the Italian Warehouse and this name can be seen on the front of the building.

LANDOWNERS AND PHILANTHROPISTS

IT IS clear from the tithe map and apportionment that up to the 1890s, the de Trafford family were by far the major landowners in Stretford. It is said that the family is one of the most ancient in the country and Ranulphus de Trafford, the earliest recorded head of the family, is mentioned in Saxon times as serving King Canute. At the time of the Norman Conquest in 1066, the de Traffords were one of the few who not only managed to retain their lands but actually increased their holdings. Ranulphus' son, also called Ranulphus, was granted land by Hamo, the Norman Barron of Dunham Massey. When William of Normandy conquered England he divided the country up into portions which he allocated to his most trusted followers. The land between the Ribble and Mersey was given to William Poitiers (this name seems to have various spellings) who, in turn, allocated some of this land to Hamo de Massey. The *Black Booke of Trafford* states that Ranulphus II and his son, Robert, received pardon and protection from Hamon de Massey, who also granted them the land of Wulfernote, a Saxon rebel. The de Traffords increased their land holding over the years by way of grants and marriages. Around 1200, in the reign of King John, Hamon de Massey, the 4th Baron of Dunham, awarded

The de Trafford family coat-of-arms. It is said that the figure with the threshing flail is that of Ranulphus de Trafford. The legend goes that he and his men were being pursued by Hammond de Massey and William the Conqueror's soldiers. Finding his cause lost, Ranulphus quickly dressed himself in the clothes of a country half-wit and hid himself in a granary near Throstle Nest ford. As Hamon and his men galloped towards the ford, he started to thresh the corn. Hamon stopped and asked if he had seen Ranulphus and his men crossing the ford, to which Ranulphus cried, 'Now thus, now thus,' on every stroke of the flail. Hamon thought he was talking to an imbecile and carried on his way. Ranulphus had saved the life of himself and his men.

Sir Edmund de Trafford IV 1526–1590. This, the fifth Edmund, married Mary, the daughter of Lord Howard and sister of Queen Catherine Howard, fifth wife of Henry VIII. He held important positions in the county, including serving three times as Sheriff of Lancashire. He was a devout Protestant and supported a large retinue in the old park at Trafford, where he provided a schoolteacher for the children of his employees and tenants.

Richard de Trafford the whole lordship of Stretford, including Trafford.

The de Trafford family has a noble lineage. Thirteen of the 25 founder members of the Order of the Garter in 1344 were predecessors of the Traffords. Sir John de Trafford, who succeeded in 1446, fought on the Lancastrian side in the Wars of the Roses. He bound himself to the Earl of Warwick to protect his lands. Around the year 1636, Sir Cecil de Trafford converted to Catholicism and some say that the family's fortunes declined because of this.

Trafford Old Hall was on the south side of Chester Road, in a sheltered garden between what is now Talbot Road and Henshaw's Society

for the Blind. The main entrance directly faced the main gate of what was once White City. The building was also known as the Moat and it is said to have been the home of the de Trafford family since c.1017. However, there is no documentation to prove this. An inventory of the effects of Sir Edmund de Trafford in 1590 said that the hall at that time had 33 rooms. Sir Cecil de Trafford bought Wickleswick Hall – known locally as 'Wiggleswick' – and estate in the mid-17th century and decided to build a new hall on the site. The estate became known as Trafford Park Estate. Trafford Park consisted of some 1,183 acres, divided into an outer park of

It'm bedds and furniture belonginge to the same xˡⁱ [xˢ]
In the backe chamber [20].
It'm one bedd and furniture to the same, xxˢ
In the bricke buyldinge [21].
It'm in bedds and all othʳ furniture belonginge, vˡⁱ
In the closett [22].
It'm one bedd and furniture for the same, xxxiijˢ iiijᵈ
In the lower bricke buyldinge [23].
It'm in beddinge and furniture to the same, xxvjˢ viijᵈ
In the chappell chamber [24].
It'm in beddinge and the furniture belonginge to the same, xlˢ
In the brewhowse chamber [25].
It'm one bedd and clothes for the same, xˢ
In the kitchin chamber [26].
It'm one bedd, xˢ
In the fawlikeners chamber [27].
It'm on bedd and furniture, xxˢ
In the horsekeeper's chamber [28].
It'm on bedd and clothes for the same, xxˢ
In the porters ward [29].
It'm in beddinge there xxvjˢ viijᵈ
In Baxter's chamber [30].
It'm one bedd and furniture, xiijˢ iiijᵈ
In Lasie his chamber [31].
I'tm in beddinge theare, xxˢ
In the schoolemʳˢ chamber [32].
It'm one bedd and furniture for the same, xxˢ
In the third chamber to Sʳ Edmound chamber [33].
· · · · · · [blank]
In the backe [bake] house, xxˢ.
In the vaie house
It'm suche furniture as beelongeth to the same, lˢ
In the kitchen
It'm in all suche furniture as beelongeth to the same, vˡⁱ
In melche cattell
It'm seven and xxxᵗⁱᵉ kyne, lxˡⁱ vjˢ viijᵈ
Younge cattell to the somme of xiijˡⁱ

Part of the inventory of Sir Edmund de Trafford, the 20th Lord of Trafford Manor. He succeeded in 1590, upon the death of his father. He was knighted by James I at York in 1603 and, like his father, was High Sheriff in 1602, 1609 and 1617.

Sir Cecil de Trafford (1599–1672) was a Justice of the Peace and said to be a persecutor of Catholics. However, in 1636, when he tried to convert Francis Downes, a relative, to the Protestant faith, he was himself converted to Catholicism, and thereafter supported the faith so strongly that he was described as an 'arch-Papist' and arrested in Manchester in 1642. From there he was taken to Kingston-upon-Hull and imprisoned in a ship 'under deck in the bottom of the ship, closer than any dungeon, in a gloomy recess without light or fresh air for several months'. Sir Cecil was eventually permitted to return to his home, where he continued to have some influence on local affairs. However, it said that the family never regained their previous standing in the country. Sir Cecil died in 1672 and was buried in the Trafford Chapel of Manchester Collegiate Church.

Sir Humphrey Francis de Trafford succeeded his father as 3d Baronet and 29th Lord of Trafford Manor, in 1886. He is seen here in his uniform as a captain in the Lancashire Hussars in 1898.

meadows and grassland through which the Bridgewater Canal was later to flow on the Chester Road side, and an inner park with a tree-lined, four-mile avenue which led to the Barton Lodge gates. The park was fairly flat, but is described as having tree-covered inclines and grassy slopes with beautiful gardens near to the hall. There were also several small sheets of water, one being known as the Lake, an oval piece of water about one eighth of a mile long with a boathouse on the west side and an island in the middle.

The family lived there until 1896, when Sir Humphrey de Trafford sold the estate to Trafford Park Estates Limited. Sir Humphrey's father served as the High Sheriff in 1861 and his marriage to Lady Mary Annette Talbot, the eldest sister and co-heiress to the 17th Earl of Shrewsbury, was said to be the first marriage since the Reformation to have been solemnized with the full Catholic ceremonial. This particular Humphrey was heavily involved in church building. In 1865, All Saints' Catholic School was built on Radcliffe Road, paid for by Sir Humphrey, as was a new Catholic church in Stretford. The building of the Manchester Ship Canal tolled the death bell for Trafford Park, however. During negotiations, Sir Humphrey's agent, Francis Ellis said that the canal would render Trafford Hall, the seat of Sir Humphrey de Trafford, uninhabitable, and he would have to 'give up his home and leave the place'.

The Duke of Bridgewater built the Bridgewater Canal, which originally was to run from the duke's Worsley mines to Hollins Ferry and Salford. However, a scheme was later devised which would take the canal through Stretford, across the Trafford Park estate, to Manchester. The duke said that the change of route was to avoid the rocky terrain that it would otherwise have to negotiate, but it is thought that the real reason was to gain easier access to the coal trade of Manchester and to enable future links with the canal routes of Cheshire. Yet the route through Trafford Park necessitated the building of the aqueduct at Barton, which was no mean feat.

However, eventually the canal was built and the de Trafford family was compensated for the inconvenience, not least with the gift of other land. A wall 9ft high was built on the Trafford Park side of the canal so as to block it off from view, and the two wharves were built solely for the use of the de Traffords. Sir Humphrey never saw the completed canal, since he died in 1886. His son, also Humphrey, succeeded him and proceeded to sell off land. In 1889 he sold part of the family lands in Davyhulme to provide a site for the new sewage works and finally, in 1896, put the estate up for auction, on Thursday 7 May that year, in the Grand Hotel, Manchester. It was thought that Manchester Council would buy the land but, after much debate, they missed the opportunity and a contract of sale between Sir Humphrey and Mr Ernest Hooley, a financier who lived at Risley Hall near Derby, was exchanged on 23 June. The total area sold was around 1,183 acres and included the land from the Manchester Ship Canal to the Bridgewater Canal. Hooley was an entrepreneur of style. He had made his money through various canny business ventures and hoped to make a big profit on Trafford Park. This he did by selling on the land – for which he had paid £36,000 – for £900,000. The new company, Trafford Parks Estates Ltd, was to be managed by Marshal Stevens, the former general manager of the Manchester Ship Canal.

One could hardly imagine the changes that would take place subsequent to the sale of the Trafford Park. One of Sir Humphrey's conditions of the sale was that the Royal Agricultural Show, which was to be held there that summer, would be allowed to proceed. This was duly done; then the park was opened to the public who enjoyed boating on the lake and picnicking on the land. It was proposed that the hall should be converted to a residential hotel, and some 80 acres devoted to the Manchester Golf Club, but the industrialisation of the area soon began and although this brought much needed work to the area, Stretford forever lost its patronage of the de Trafford family. A small village was built in the middle of the park to house the workers. To the first inhabitants it was like living in the countryside, but the big companies soon changed all that and a thriving community with

Trafford Old Hall was situated on Chester Road opposite the gates of White City. The building was originally a black and white timbered structure which was later plastered over. In 1590 it is said to have had 33 rooms, and the hearth tax in 1673 gives 33 hearths. The hall had an uninterrupted view of the River Irwell through to Ordsall Hall on the other side, and was said to have an underground passage to this hall (*Manchester City News*, November 1909). Harrison Ainsworth mentions Trafford Old Hall in his book *Guy Fawkes*. The building was demolished in 1939.

a school and church evolved. Trafford Hall was left empty for many years before being demolished during World War Two. The Trafford Centre now stands on the land.

One of the more recent and most notable benefactors of Stretford was John Rylands. He was born in St Helens in 1801, where his father was a linen manufacturer. At the age of 16 John joined his father in the trade. Obviously a budding entrepreneur, he made his first private profits after buying a drawer of old jewellery at an auction, dismantling it, and selling it on at a much inflated price. He then used this money to buy yarn and had it woven by his mother's

former nurse and her family. The resulting cloth was sold at quite a handsome profit. Eventually, in 1823, John Rylands came to Manchester and opened a warehouse in High Street. From then on his career flourished and over a span of 50 years he had built up a company with his sons worth £2 million.

Mr Rylands bought Longford Hall in 1855, from Charles James Stanley Walker. Charles's father, Thomas Walker, who was borough reeve of Manchester, had lived in the hall until his death. This gentleman seems to have been a colourful character who was keen on reform and not afraid to stand up for his principles. At one

Trafford Hall, 1905. This hall was built by Sir Cecil de Trafford on the site of Wickleswick Hall. It occupied a good position on a slightly elevated site and was a spacious building with an impressive frontage. The gardens were extensive and beautifully laid out and in this photograph we can see what looks like a garden party in progress, although all the guests seem to be male. There is a bus at the far right-hand edge.

point he fell victim to his enemies and was arraigned at Lancaster Assizes on a charge of High Treason. He was, however, honorably acquitted. It would seem that daring ran in the family, as it was a lady of the same family who was the first to use an umbrella in Manchester, being much jostled and derided for doing so. John Rylands demolished the old house and built a mansion in which he lived from 1857 until his death in December 1888, having been married three times and producing two surviving children.

Mr Rylands's interests were diverse and not merely money-orientated. He accomplished much during his life in Stretford. In 1865 he took a leading role of the erection of the Union

Church for Congregationalists, of which he was a member, and established homes for aged gentlewomen. Rylands was responsible for the establishment of many public buildings, institutions and facilities such as the public baths, the comprehensively stocked public library, a coffee house and the Longford Institute with its bowling green, tennis court and children's playground situated next to the Town Hall.

Rylands was also a notable public figure. In 1857 he served as High Constable of the Salford Hundred and in 1869 was made a Justice of the Peace for Lancashire.

John Rylands seems to have been a man of great energy. He edited a bible which was issued

After the sale of Trafford Hall in 1896, and until the first of the developers moved into the park, a number of schemes were considered in order to make the estate a paying concern. One of these schemes was to let 80 acres nearest the hall to the Manchester Golf Club. This move by the club to Trafford Park was very successful and membership rose from 70 to 320. Members were allowed to use part of the hall, and those who were employed by the new industries moving into the park benefited from a reduced subscription to the golf club.

Carriageway to Trafford Hall c.1895. The avenue to the hall was lined with trees, most of which were lime and sycamore. E. Mills, in his description of the avenue and grounds of Trafford Hall, paints an idyllic scene: 'Flying among the trees were linnets, thrushes, blackbirds, willow-wrens, finches, swallows, and many others singing their full-throated songs to their hearts' content.' The sign on the gatepost stated that the hall is closed to the public.

This portrait of John Rylands (1801–1888) formerly hung at Longford Hall.

a director. Mr Rylands's wife, Enriqueta, survived him and continued many of his good works. She was given the freedom of Manchester upon the opening of the John Rylands Library which she commissioned to be built in Deansgate as a lasting tribute to her husband. Mrs Rylands died in 1908 and Longford Hall and estate was sold to Stretford Council in 1911, after a poll of ratepayers. In 1912 the park was opened to the public. The house was eventually demolished as it became unsafe.

LONGFORD ESTATE.

TO BE SOLD BY AUCTION,

BY MR. WM. GRUNDY,

AT THE CLARENCE HOTEL, SPRING GARDENS,
MANCHESTER,

On THURSDAY the 14th DAY of OCTOBER,
And not on Thursday the 24th of Sept., as previously advertised,

(*Subject to such conditions of sale as will be then and there produced.*)

THE SALE TO COMMENCE AT SIX O'CLOCK IN THE EVENING, PRECISELY,

LOT 1.—ALL THAT

MESSUAGE, OR MANSION,

Commonly called or known by the name of LONGFORD HALL, together with the Coach Houses, Stables, Cow Houses, Sheds, and other Out-Buildings, Garden, Orchard, Plantations, and Shrubberies, thereto belonging, and occupied therewith. And also all those several Closes, Closures, Fields, or

PARCELS OF LAND,

Situate and being in the townships of Stretford and Chorlton-with-Hardy, in the County of Lancaster, commonly called by the several names of the Further Brook Meadow, or Far Black Meadow; the Near Brook Meadow, or Brook Field; the Adams Field; the Coat Field, or Four Acre; the Cow Lane Head, or the Carr Lane Head; the Parson's Acre; the Hawthorn Meadow, or the Little Hawthorn; and the Baguley Acre; which said Closes of Land contain together in the whole (including the site of the said Messuage or Mansion House, Buildings, Garden, and Orchard,) 29A. 3R. 7P. of Land, Lancashire Measure, or thereabouts, be the same more or less, and are now in the occupation of Charles James Stanley Walker, Esquire.

LOT 2.

ALL THAT FIELD OR PARCEL OF LAND,

Part of which is now occupied as a Garden. Together with the Cottage or Dwelling House erected thereon, situate in the said Township of Chorlton-with-Hardy, containing 3A. 33P. of Land, Lancashire Measure, or thereabouts, be the same more or less, and now in the occupation of the said Charles James Stanley Walker, Esquire.

The above Premises are Freehold of Inheritance, and Lot 1 will be sold subject to the payment of the yearly rent of £160.

Longford Hall is situate about four miles from Manchester, within five minutes' walk of the Stretford Station of the Manchester, Altrincham, and Bowdon Railway, and is a desirable residence for a respectable family.

The Land is in a high state of cultivation, and the Gardens (one of which is walled round) and Orchard are well stocked with choice Fruit Trees which are very productive.

The Land adjoining Longford Hall is surrounded with a Plantation, and is very eligible for Building purposes.

For further particulars, application may be made at the Offices of the Auctioneer, Savings' Bank Buildings, or Messrs. T. A. & J. GRUNDY, Solicitors, 63, King Street, Manchester, where a Plan of the Estate may be seen.

Notice of the sale of Longford Hall in 1852. The hall had been owned previously by Thomas Walker, who inherited it from his father, also Thomas, on his death in 1817. The younger Thomas died in 1836 and his brother, Charles, spent much time and money in converting the small house and fields into a mansion and park. He was still in occupation when the estate was offered by auction in 1852.

in three volumes in 1863, 1878, and 1886, the index for which was said to be the most detailed and clear in existence. At the age of 70 he decided to learn Italian, probably because he bought a house in Trastevere in Italy. His generosity also extended to that country where he maintained an orphanage. The King of Italy rewarded him for his work with the children by conferring upon him the title of Knight of the Order of the Crown of Italy.

Mr Rylands died in 1888 at the age of 87 and was buried at Manchester Southern Cemetery. Reubin Spence, who lived at Darley Hall, Seymour Grove, was associated with Rylands & Sons for 50 years. When John Rylands died, Spence took over the firm where he had previously been

Above and below: Longford Hall and gates. John Rylands bought the Longford Estate and Hall in 1855. He demolished the existing hall and built a mansion more to his own taste. He died at Longford Hall in 1888, his wife surviving him by 20 years.

RENT AND RATE-PAYERS OF STRETFORD.

Vote in favour of the purchase of Longford Hall Estate.

BECAUSE:

1. Parks and Open Spaces mean improved health, recreation and comfort of the community.

2. The price of Longford Park is admittedly cheap. The cost of purchase, £14,500, will involve an Annual Charge of £694, but ratepayers should not overlook the fact that the Estate comprises property which to-day produces £537 per annum, thereby reducing the cost of purchase on the rates to £157 per annum. The fringe of the Estate, if sold for villa residences at the low price of one penny per yard will produce £225 per annum in perpetuity, and consequently the remainder of the Estate (43 acres) will become the property of the ratepayers free of cost.

3. If the ratepayers miss this one opportunity they will have to pay for Open Spaces four times the cost per acre when the district develops in the near future.

4. It is not true that your rents will greatly increase. The charge per house is very small, indeed the facts are that on a house rented at from 5/- to 7/6 per week, the cost to the tenant will be less than a farthing per week, and up to a rental of 12/- per week the cost to the tenant will be less than a halfpenny per week.

5. The only charge the ratepayers will have to bear will be that of adaptation and maintenance. The estimate made by the Council is ample beyond dispute, it being based on the experience of the cost of the Parks in the district. The rate (less than one penny) will not increase but, on the contrary, will decrease in proportion as the rateable value increases.

RATEPAYERS, do not fail to accept this golden opportunity of providing a natural woodland park for your children and yourselves and support your representatives who desire to make the conditions of life for you and your successors healthier and brighter.

Do not fill up your Voting Paper until you have had an opportunity either of seeing the Park or hearing your representatives at Public Meetings to be held this week.

THE PARK IS NOW OPEN FOR INSPECTION.

JAMES WILLIAMS - - - *Chairman of the Council.*
C. H. SENIOR - - *Deputy-Chairman of the Council.*

MEMBERS OF THE COUNCIL.

R. G. BAGLEY.	JAMES LAMB.
F. W. BATES.	JAMES MARPLE.
EDWARD COLLENS.	JOHN ROBERTS.
JAMES FAULKNER.	THOMAS ROBINSON.
F. W. GOULD.	HENRY STOTHARD.
THOMAS JOHNSTON.	CHARLES TAYLOR.
JOHN KELSALL.	JOHN WHITESIDE.

February 14th, 1911.

James Bent, who lived at Northumberland House, Old Trafford, was a well-known figure in Stretford in the first half of the 19th century. He was superintendent of the Manchester Police from 1868 until his death in 1901. A brave, strong man, he was known for his strength of spirit and for encouraging that of his officers. To this end he organised annual sports days and social events to reinforce team spirit within his force.

Bent was the originator of a soup kitchen for poor children, and of a scheme to distribute warm clothing among the poor of the area. It was for these activities, perhaps more than any of his other achievements, that he is best remembered. The soup kitchen survived until the end of World War One.

In 1911 Stretford Borough Council bought the Longford Estate after a poll of ratepayers was held to consult public opinion.

In 1912, a ceremony marked the opening of Longford Park to the public. The three centre figures are Lady Robinson, Sir Thomas Robinson and Harry Nuttall MP.

Longford Hall after its opening to the public. This is a busy scene and clearly the people of the area took full advantage of this enjoyable park. At one time the building housed the local authority's art collection. The hall and park continued to play an important role in the history of Stretford, acting as the venue for many public events, even after the hall itself was demolished.

Longford Hall, the scene of many important local events. This photograph shows Lord Derby presenting the Charter for Stretford in front of the hall.

Longford Park and the round conservatory.

Longford Park School, pictured in 1931.

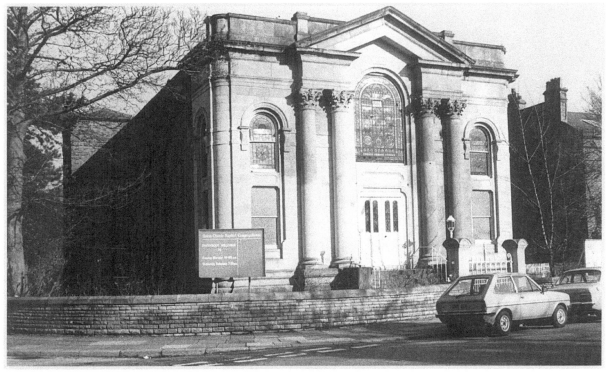

The Union Church, Edge Lane, was built by John Rylands. In 1865 a number of people, most of whom were members of the Congregational church, met at the Town Hall and became founder members of the Union Church. On 2 January 1867 John Rylands, who was a trustee, laid the foundation stone of the church, and the first service took place the following year.

Chester Road looking from Market Street, with the Longford Coffee House, built by John Rylands, on the corner.

Darley Hall, Seymour Grove, the home of Reubin Spence, who was a director of John Rylands's firm. It was a stone building in the Tudor style, standing in grounds of about eight acres. Mr Spence died in 1901 and houses now stand on the land.

Hullard Park, 1951. In 1786 the *Manchester Mercury* advertised: 'Hullart Hall is to let with the lands thereto belonging containing 107 and a half acres of Lancashire measure now in the occupation of Widow Newton.' The word 'hullart' means 'owlet'. By 1860, the occupant was Mr Ernest Bates and the barn belonging to the house had been converted into cottages, as can be seen on the 1876 Ordnance Survey map of the area. By the time of the 1908 survey, the area had become a park. This was the first park to be opened by the local authorities.

Superintendent James Bent, who served in the Lancashire Constabulary. He was appointed to this post on 16 April 1848 and held it until his death on 8 July 1901. He sustained fearful injuries in an attack at a steelworks in Miles Platting, when an attempt was made to burn out his tongue with hot irons, but his fighting spirit enabled him to carry on with his career, despite subsequent health problems which dogged him until his death.

Stretford Borough Councillors, 1904–5. Those named are J.W. Doran, Lamb, J. Marple, Hogan, Thos Johnson, J. Roberts, F.W. Bates, F.W. Gould, J. Whiteside, Williams, J. Kelsall, C.H. Senior, H. Stothard, H. Lewtas, J. Faulkner, T. Robinson, E. Collins, T.W. Finney, C. Taylor and G.H. Brown. This information has been taken from the back of the photograph and is unfortunately incomplete.

HOUSING AND
LOCAL SERVICES

U P UNTIL the 19th century the rural land-scape of Stretford had remained relat-ively unchanged for centuries, but from the early 1800s the Industrial Revolution, along with improvements in the transport system, brought about great changes. The introduction of canals during the 18th century and the railways in the 19th century had produced cheaper transport costs, enabling the expansion of industry nationwide. This brought with it a

Trafford Town Hall was used by Stretford Council and was lit by gas burners until 1902. It was enlarged in 1907 to include a larger council chamber. The committee rooms were centered around a central stairway, which then had corridors leading to the various council departments.

Old Trafford County Modern Secondary School for Boys was designed by Mr Percy Howard and opened in January 1930. The school had a novel central heating system, which was connected to the cloakroom rails so that any wet clothes and coats would dry quickly.

demand for more housing, as people in search of work migrated to areas where work was more plentiful. The rural landscape of Stretford began to change to a more urban one, with houses and streets replacing the open fields and farmland. The houses, which were built during the construction of the Bridgewater Canal and the Manchester South Junction Railway, provided utilitarian terraced homes for the workers. These also included lodging houses, which could accommodate 20 to 30 people at a time and provided temporary accommodation for groups of travelling workers who would move on when the job was completed.

This urbanisation, which had begun during

the early 19th century, accelerated as the century moved on. The population during this period was also on the increase and this in turn created further demands on the environment. As we have seen earlier, in the 1800s rural Stretford consisted of small areas of housing with two densely populated areas. One was around St Matthew's Church and the other was located in the Old Trafford area, where the road names included Derbyshire Lane, Old Lane, Stretford New Road, Back Lane, Edge Lane and Trafford Lane. By 1890, although the two separate areas are still identifiable, the landscape had altered considerably. Large amounts of open land had been replaced by new housing development.

This building was built by Mr John Rylands in 1878 and was often referred to as the 'Town Hall' although it was not used for any administrative purpose. After the death of John Rylands, Stretford Council bought the building for £5,000. The main hall included a library and classrooms and was used primarily for educational purposes. Attached to the main building was a swimming bath.

Members of the Stretford Fire Brigade are seen here on Charter Day in 1933, taking part in the celebrations to mark the Royal Charter which bestowed upon Stretford the status of a municipal borough.

Five Ways roundabout, seen here in 1957, was one of the main entry and exit points for the workforce of Trafford Park. At the time this photograph was taken, most people either travelled to work by public transport or by cycle. Few could afford the luxury of a car. The number of buses heading away from the Trafford Park area indicates that this photograph was taken at the end of a working day.

Moss Park Junior School, seen here in 1951, was opened in 1930 and situated on Moss Park Road. The school was built to accommodate the influx of people to the area as a result of the new housing estate on Derbyshire Lane West. The infants' school was built in 1934.

Chester Road, looking towards City Road, in 1923 was still cobbled and, on this photograph, looks very dirty. The building, which can be seen on the left of the photograph is Duckworth's Essence factory and which is still in existence today, while the Northumberland public house is just visible on the far right.

This photograph of Lacy Street, which was taken in August 1971, shows that the street lighting is of an older type and had not yet been modernised. The Longford Essoldo cinema is just visible in the distance, although by then it was advertising bingo.

Rows of terraced houses began to appear, especially in the area along either side of Stretford Road, starting from St Matthew's Church and reaching as far as Longford Bridge. Roads such as King Street, Brunswick Street, Church Street and Wellington Street had been built and Trafford Lane in Old Trafford had been renamed Seymour Grove. The houses in the Seymour Grove area were built in a grand style with large gardens, their names reflected their status – the Beeches, the Limes, the Elms, the Sycamores and Skelton House. These villa-type houses provided homes for the wealthy city businessmen who wanted to live in a desirable area, but remain close to Manchester city centre. The area around Seymour Grove became a fashionable place to live and provided residents with large recreational areas such as the Manchester County Gun Club, the Lancashire County Cricket Club, the Manchester Polo Club, the Old Trafford Bowling Club and the Royal Botanical Gardens.

Closer to Old Trafford's border with Manchester, the housing was much more densely packed with rows and rows of back-to-backs. Shrewsbury Street, Barrett Street and Henrietta Street had all been built, and the area was a tight-knit working-class community

Stretford Road, which can be seen here in 1923, was still cobbled and, despite the improvements to transport which had taken place, the cobbles provided a difficult surface. The horse and cart was still a regular form of transport for carrying goods and services, despite the introduction of the motor vehicle some years earlier. This photograph has been taken looking towards Trafford Bar.

consisting mainly of terraced housing, which was in direct contrast to the wealthy area around Seymour Grove. The census for 1891 indicates the types of occupation carried out by some of the inhabitants of Shrewsbury Street in Old Trafford and included a policemen, warehouseman, servant and clerk.

The industrial expansion and urbanisation, which followed the departure of the de Trafford family after the building of the Manchester Ship Canal, had already been developing for some time but now continued at a much more rapid pace. The same could be said for the provision of goods and services.

The population of Stretford increased to such an extent that in 1801 it stood at 1,477, in 1851 it was 4,998, but by 1901 this had risen to 30,436. This continual rise created demands on local government, transport, heating, lighting, schools, the fire service and the police, all of which had to adapt very quickly.

Local Government had previously been under the jurisdiction of the parish vestry who dealt with the administration of the Poor Law and other civil matters. Their role was often a confusing one and, as urban growth took a hold, they quickly became outmoded and were replaced. Stretford Local Board was created in

1867 and took over the role of governing the following year. The first offices were based at 5 Windsor Terrace (later renumbered 534 Chester Road), which were located opposite Trafford Bar. In 1887 new premises were built on Talbot Road. These had been especially designed for the purpose by Mr Colin C, McLeod, of Greenheys, at a cost of £4,000. The new building was constructed of red brick, stone and terracotta. The local board continued its role of governing until 1894, when it was superseded by Stretford Urban District Council. The local board, and later Stretford UDC, were responsible for the upkeep and maintenance of highways, sanitation, school attendance and the cemetery. They set local rates, which were levied on property to raise money to provide for the maintenance of these services.

Transport links continued to improve and the construction of the first tramways started in Salford in 1861. By 1877 the Manchester and Salford Tramways began construction on lines linking Stretford Road, City Road, Chester Road and Chorlton Road. By 1880 services were running from Piccadilly to Old Trafford via Chester Road. The first trams were pulled by horses and could accommodate up to 41 people. They were painted red and cream with stairs, which were situated at the rear of the vehicle, leading to the top deck. The top deck of the tram was uncovered, similar to the horse-drawn coach, and would have been priced at a cheaper rate than inside. The trams travelled at a rate of 6mph and the journey from Manchester to Stretford could take anything up to two hours as the route had no fixed stops until after the

The Royal Residential School for the Deaf was originally located in Stanley Street in Salford but the premises had proved too small and a larger building was required. The cost of the new school was £10,000. A grand bazaar and a ball raised £3,900 to help with cost. The school was designed by Mr Richard Lane and was opened to pupils in 1837. The first master was Mr William Vaughan.

Stamford Street, Old Trafford, was one of the many streets which began to spring up in the Old Trafford area during the late 19th century. The streets were of a uniform nature, almost regimented in design. The houses provided homes for people who worked in the city of Manchester. The 1881 census indicates that some of the houses, such as number 11 and 13, were still under construction. The occupations of the residents of Stamford Street included those of a commercial clerk, a cashier, an architect and a law stationer.

1880s. The driver would stop the tram for anyone who wanted to get on or off. The tram driver had to control the horse with one hand holding the reins, while the other hand would control the brake. In 1900, Manchester Corporation bought out the company for the sum of £73,149 and made the decision to electrify the trams, eventually extending the line to run all the way to Altrincham.

Originally it fell to the church to provide education for the parish and one of the early references to a school in Stretford was the marriage of the local schoolmaster Mr Simon Kearsley of Leigh in 1656. In 1708, the Court Baron refers to a Mrs Clayton as the school-mistress. Pupils were expected to pay fees to attend school, but many children did not attend

as they were too poor. In 1724, as a result of a bequest from Mrs Ann Hinde, the widow of John Hinde, the minister of Stretford (1696–1701), clothing and education was to be provided for 20 poor children aged 8 to 11 years. Mrs Hinde stipulated that boys should wear green frocks, green vests and green stockings, and for girls, green gowns, caps, handkerchiefs, stockings and shoes. Not surprisingly, the children who attended the school became known as the green scholars.

Early schools taught pupils by rote under the supervision of monitors and it was not until 1846 that the pupil-teacher system was set up, which stated that a teacher had to serve an apprenticeship of five years before teaching. The 1870 Education Act made the provision of

This aerial picture of Brooks Bar in 1926 gives a good overview of the area. The road which can be seen from the foreground is Upper Chorlton Road.

schools compulsory in areas where non-existed, but it was not until 1876 that school attendance became compulsory throughout. Stretford School Attendance Committee met for the first time on 5 June 1877.

The increase in population put great pressure on the schools themselves, which in many areas were overcrowded and dirty. A parent from Derbyshire Lane in Stretford refused to send his child to a school because it was 'dirty, overcrowded and insanitary'. Some schools were private and worked on a fee-paying basis, providing education for the children of more wealthy parents. Most of these were day schools,

but some were boarding schools, such as Elmswood College which was run by Miss Sloman and Miss Webb and situated on Cromwell Street in Stretford, close to Edge Lane. Private schools came and went as demand dictated; one of the last in the area was that of Brook High School which closed in 1930.

There were two charity-funded schools in Old Trafford, the Royal Residential School for the Deaf and Henshaw's School for the Blind, which catered for children across the north-west.

The fire service originally comprised employees of the local authority who worked in various departments, and only worked in the fire

Chester Road, White City, in 1905. The railings which can be seen on the left of the photograph are those of Henshaw's Blind Asylum.

Seymour Park Council School was opened in 1907 by Councillor Estcourt. The school cost £12,450 and provided places for 300 infants and 540 junior pupils.

Chester Road, seen here looking towards King Street with the Longford Coffee House on the left. The gentleman on the bicycle is thought to be the local doctor, Dr Andrew Westwood.

service on a part-time basis when the need arose. All the fire-fighting equipment was stored next to Stretford police station and consisted of a hose-cart with pipes, which had to be pushed by the men themselves. In 1939 the fire service was established as a full-time concern and was administered by the Stretford and Urmston Joint Fire Brigade Committee. The new fire station was built on Park Road where it remains today. The station also included houses to accommodate the firemen, and a modern fire-fighting vehicle.

Rural Stretford could be a hazardous area, and policing it was often difficult. The area around Throstle Nest, close to the Cornbrook area, was a favourite haunt of thieves and

robbers and, in November 1803, the *Manchester Mercury* reported: 'Thomas Aldred of Urmston has been robbed of £800 and shot dead by highwaymen'. In 1839, Stretford came under the Lancashire Constabulary and, for the first time, had a professional police force. The policemen wore a uniform which consisted of a top hat, blue tailcoat and blue or white trousers. Whistles were first used in 1859 and the cockscomb helmets were issued in 1864. A policeman's life was not an easy one, and was often violent, resulting in injuries and, in many cases, death. In 1857 the scale of pay was 17s 6d (88p) per week for a third-class constable rising to 19s 6d for a first-class constable. Policemen were also expected to obtain permission before they

Chester Road, looking towards Manchester. The tram is of the horse-drawn variety. The photograph is thought to have been taken around 1898.

married. On 9 September 1899, Kay Hoyle, a policeman serving with the Manchester Division of the Lancashire Constabulary at Stretford, received permission to marry Harriet Jones of Chorlton cum Hardy.

During the 20th century the urban development of Stretford continued. Trafford Park as an industrial area was continuing to expand and during the late 1920s and early 1930s, semi-detached housing and council housing began to fill in the gaps in open spaces, finally linking the whole of the Stretford area together. During the 1920s, Stretford had been petitioning for a charter which would give them borough status and allow them to be self-governing. This was granted and, on 16 September 1933, Stretford

Stretford Grammar School for Boys was opened in 1929. It was situated on Great Stone Road and provided places for 470 pupils. The school was extended in the 1930s to include a new library, and in 1957 a new dining room was also added.

This photograph of Chester Road was taken from opposite St Matthew's Church and shows the spire of the Congregational Church, which was taken down during the 1950s. The motor vehicle bears the number plate B485, which indicates the photograph was probably taken around 1904.

finally became a municipal borough. Lord Derby handed over the charter to the new mayor during the opening ceremony of the new Town Hall, which had been built on Talbot Road. Sir Thomas Robinson, who had served as the MP for Stretford for 13 years and had also been a member of the Urban District Council, held the office of the first mayor.

As we shall see later, World War Two brought great destruction to the Stretford area, especially around Moss Lane and Trafford Park, which was a particular target of German bomber pilots. In the period following the war, new housing development took place in areas which had been affected by the bombing.

Brooks Bar around 1880, looking towards Moss Lane West. This junction was very busy with horse-drawn trams, carriages and even cattle.

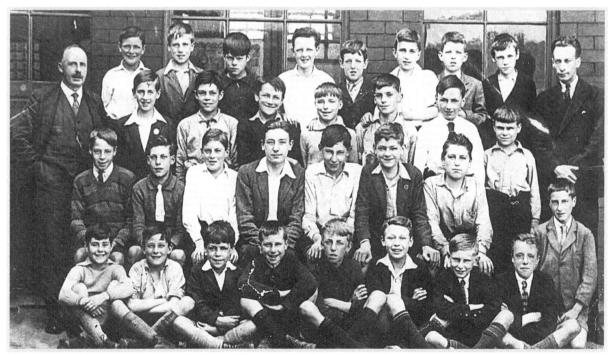

Victoria Park School in 1923. The school was situated in Henshaw Street and opened in 1905. It was extended in 1907 to provide places for 200 mixed infants and 400 mixed juniors. This photograph shows the headmaster, Mr Charles Mottram, on the left with Mr Howard West on the right.

Lancashire Constabulary pictured in the yard of the Old Trafford police station in 1900.

Shrewsbury Street, seen here in 1923, was lined with large Victorian houses and may have derived its name from the Earl of Shrewsbury, who was connected to the de Trafford family through the marriage of his sister, Mary Annette Talbot, to Sir Humphrey de Trafford.

Cemetery Lodge stood in the grounds of the cemetery and was the home of the Stretford registrar. Stretford Local Board opened Stretford cemetery on 7 April 1885.

Henshaw's Institute for the Blind was opened in 1839 and was linked to the Deaf and Dumb School by the chapel of St Thomas's. The money for the school had been provided by Thomas Henshaw who, in a codicil to his will dated 9 January 1808, left £20,000 for the provision of a Blind Institution.

The opening of the Lostock housing estate on Barton Road in 1931.

The police station located on King Street had been built to replace an earlier one which had been taken down in 1897. This photograph was taken in 1959. The main police headquarters are now on Talbot Road.

Gorse Hill Council School was opened in 1910. The pupils seen in this photograph are receiving prizes from Councillor Dorran.

During the 1960s and '70s, many local authorities began to provide high-rise flats as an answer to the housing shortage. Osprey Court on Clifford Street, Old Trafford, was opened in 1970.

Mitford Street houses are a good example of the regimental type of housing that was built in the late 1800s. These houses are pictured looking towards Cyprus Street and were photographed just before demolition.

Chadwick Cottages on Derbyshire Lane were built with only one door to each dwelling. They were known as 'through houses' and these are pictured in 1937. Note the open drain which ran through the alleyway.

Brunswick Street looking towards Chester Road. The cottages are a mixture of old and new, with both thatched and tiled roofs.

The white house which can be seen in the middle of this photograph of Chapel Lane was known as Dick Radcliff's Cottage.

The motorway brought about great changes to the local landscape and this photograph, taken in 1972, shows the motorway bridge at Chester Road under construction. Looking towards Sale, the offices of Dane Road can just be seen.

Pupils from Victoria Park Council School, Stretford, are seen here with the headmaster Mr C. Mottram in 1908.

IN PURSUIT OF LEISURE

THROUGHOUT history, leisure time has always played an important role in everyday life. Many early festivals and celebrations were centered on the church calendar, especially saints' days. The week-long Stretford Wakes, which was one such religious festival, began on the first Sunday following the first week in October each year. Festivities would include, morris and maypole dancing, sideshows, stalls, games and feasting. In 1843, during the

The Ould Band pictured in Nunnery Gardens on the Isle of Man in 1865, where they played at the official opening. The Ould Band was the predecessor of the Temperance Band. There were some earlier bands, such as the Village and the Church Bands, which were formed in 1877 and 1879 respectively, but prior to this date there is no record of any other. Band members in the photograph include John Mellor, David Kelsall, George Foster, George Kelsall (leader), Joseph Kelsall, John Hancock, William Holt, John Royle, John Kelsall, John Pixton and William Jones. John Pixton, who is pictured fourth from the right (with hand on hip) is described on the back of the photograph as a 'pig killer'.

The Stretford Village Band performing in Victoria Park in 1910.

The Primitive Methodist Chapel choir enjoying a picnic during the early 1900s.

During the early 1900s, St Peter's Church in Stretford held their annual Rose Queen Festival and an open-air fête, which was a forerunner of the Stretford pageant that we are familiar with today. This picture shows the event at Gorse Hill Farm, Longford Bridge, on Saturday 20 August 1910. Admission was 6d and the use of the stands and chairs incurred an extra charge The grand parade included morris dancers, children from the Heath House orphanage and the band of the 8th Battalion Lancashire Fusiliers. There was also a fancy dress display. The procession started from Gorse Hill Council School yard and proceeded to the field via Cavendish Road, Nansen Street, Taylor's Road, Chester Road, Derbyshire Lane, Cyprus Street, School Road and finally King Street. There were also sports including a tug-of-war, a pierrot concert, dancing and a bonny baby show. This all culminated in the crowning of the Rose Queen, Miss Gladys Boyling.

consecration of St Matthew's Church, Sir Thomas de Trafford peeped into the church to see if more people were attending the service than were at the Wakes horse racing he was staging on a racecourse next to Crossford Bridge.

There was usually bear-baiting and cock-fighting and the festivities would often go on into the evenings. In 1868, Stretford Local Board decided that the nature of the Wakes had changed so much in character that they imposed restrictions on stallholders and charged for pitches to discourage the Wakes from taking place at all. The Wakes slowly died out, although in some parts of the country the tradition still survives.

Whit week was another religious festival and was celebrated with a procession of witness, in which children and members of the congregation would parade through the streets to witness their faith. A local band, followed by members of the congregation carrying embroidered banners, would lead the parade. In Stretford, children from the Nonconformist churches would hold their walk on a Wednesday, while children from the Church of England would walk the following day. The children would be dressed in their best clothes and, at various points along the route, would stop and sing hymns. After tea, which was usually held in the Sunday school, the children would change into

Miss Dorothy Brown, Stretford's Rose Queen in 1911.

grounds, football grounds and bowling greens were numerous.

The Botanical and Horticultural Society Gardens, which covered an area of over 16 acres, were opened to the public in 1831. The gardens included several large glasshouses where a variety of tropical plants were grown. In Victorian times it became fashionable for the ladies and gentlemen of the day to arrive in horse-drawn carriages and parade around the grounds. In 1857 the gardens played host to the Art Treasures Exhibition, a prestigious event opened by Queen Victoria's consort, Prince Albert. New iron buildings were specially erected for the exhibition at a cost of £38,000, and the prince was so enamoured of the exhibition that a month after his visit he returned again, this time bringing Victoria and the rest of his family. The exhibition ran for a total of 142 days and was visited by over 1,336,700 people, including Alfred Lord Tennyson and Prince Napoleon. In 1887 the site was chosen as a venue for the Royal Jubilee Exhibition to commemorate 50 years of Queen Victoria's reign. The plans for the exhibition meant that the site had to be extended as far as Talbot Road and Warwick Road. The main building was shaped like a cross and measured 1,000ft in length and included a dome measuring 140ft high at the centre. The architects chosen to carry out the work were Maxwell & Tuke, who later built Blackpool Tower. The Prince of Wales opened the exhibition accompanied by the Prime Minister, Mr W.E. Gladstone. The exhibition lasted a total of 192 days and was attended by 4,765,000 people; on one day alone the attendance figure reached a staggering 74,000. The gardens gradually fell into disuse and in 1907 they were sold to White

their everyday clothes in order to play games. Trips to the seaside or the countryside were arranged for some of the older children.

It was during the Victorian period that leisure became more popular. The Victorians enjoyed outdoor sport, and 'taking the air' was a popular pastime, although for many working-class people, leisure activity was limited to what little free time and money they had available. It was also during this period that many of our parks and gardens were built, where people could take a stroll or listen to the local band on a Sunday afternoon. In the early part of the 19th century, the area around Seymour Grove had already become popular with the middle classes. Cricket

Stretford pageant celebrations in Longford Park during the 1920s. The bandstand was once a popular venue for the local band, especially on Sunday afternoons. Although the bandstand is no longer situated in the ground of Longford Park, it has been carefully restored and can now be seen at the Crich Tramway Village, home of the National Tramway Museum, in Derbyshire. Longford Hall is just visible in the background.

City Entertainments, who transformed the site into an entertainment resort. The great exhibition hall was turned into a restaurant and the rest of the buildings utilised to provide a dance hall and a skating rink. The palm house, including the giant palm trees, became a tearoom where visitors could marvel at the unique surroundings. A scenic railroad, water chute and a helter-skelter were also built, along with daily displays and bands to provide entertainment during the summer months. The cost of admission was 6d and the park was open daily from 12.30pm until 11pm. During the

month of June 1907, a flower show was held which included the added attraction of 10,000 electric lights and which was described as 'A Veritable Fairyland'. All the forthcoming events were advertised weekly in the *Stretford Telegraph*. However, concern was soon raised that the site was becoming 'Americanised'. This was strongly denied by the management, who maintained that the White City would always retain its English character. The park prospered for a while and, in September 1907, every one of its 600 staff were taken for a day out to Blackpool. They travelled by train, leaving

Stretford pageant in 1920, showing the crowning of the Rose Queen, Miss Dora Gresty.

Victoria Station in Manchester around 10am and were treated to lunch in one of the largest restaurants in Blackpool. The party enjoyed a full day at the seaside before returning to Stretford on the 9pm train that evening. Unfortunately, the success of the White City Entertainment Park did not last for long and by March 1914 it was closed.

World War One saw some of the buildings used as warehouses, and when peace was

Lord Derby with the Rose Queen, Miss Mildred Appleton, at the 1942 Stretford pageant. The pageant included a grand procession which started out from Hullard Park at 2.30pm and proceeded to Longford Park via Henrietta Street, Ayres Road, Skerton Road, King's Road, the Quadrant, Great Stone Road, Chester Road and Edge Lane. Seats for the crowning ceremony cost 1s for a front-row seat and 6d for those behind.

Coronations and royal celebrations have always provided an outlet for street entertainment. The coronation of Edward VII in 1902 provided the residents of the appropriately-named King Street with this cheerful display.

restored there were some attempts to hold exhibitions there, but these came to nothing. In 1917 the Palm House was demolished and some of the land was sold to the Trustees of the Royal School for the Deaf and Dumb.

Eventually White City was converted to a greyhound-racing track, before it was finally demolished altogether during the latter part of the 20th century. At the time of writing, all that remains of the Botanical Gardens is Botanical Road and the old entrance gates, which have been carefully renovated and stand on display close to the entrance of what is today the White City retail park.

The Pomona Gardens were situated on the banks of the River Irwell close to where the Pomona Docks are today, and covered an area of around 21 acres which included a large lake. An annual regatta was held on the Irwell and rowers would compete singly or in teams of eight. During the summer months, pleasure craft could be hired to row along the river. In 1849 a show was held in the gardens in which the eruption of Mount Vesuvius was depicted on a large canvas. The gardens eventually fell into disrepair and were bought by Mr James Reilly in 1868. He was responsible for improving the gardens and building a large hall or 'Palace' as it was known. The hall covered an area of 45,800 square feet and could hold up to 28,000 people. Dances and

Another royal celebration, albeit some 75 years later. During the Queen's silver jubilee in 1977, street parties were a popular way of marking the event. This one was held in the Milton Road area of Stretford.

Children at the gates of Victoria Park during the 1970s.

These two views of Victoria Park – one of the bowling green, the other of the floral display – indicate how grand public parks used to be. The photographs were taken during the early 1900s when bowling was a popular sport for both ladies and gentlemen. The park measured around 19 acres and also provided tennis courts and other recreational facilities.

Children playing in Longford Park some time during the late 1970s.

entertainments were held there, and the great political orator Benjamin Disraeli addressed two political meetings there. The buildings were demolished during the construction of the Manchester Ship Canal.

Spectator sports were becoming popular and there were many cricket grounds in the area, but the most famous – the headquarters of Lancashire County Cricket Club – is the one we all think of in association with Stretford. It was originally sited behind the Botanical Gardens but when they were extended during the exhibition of 1857, the ground was moved to its present site on Warwick Road. The world-famous red brick pavilion was built in 1884, although it has been altered many times since then. By the end of the 19th century, football was a major spectator sport. Manchester United

originally began life around 1878 as a small works club, drawing its players from the carriage and wagon department of the Lancashire & Yorkshire Railway based at Newton Heath. They eventually moved to a ground at Bank Lane, Clayton, before switching to their present ground at Old Trafford in 1910. They had adopted the title of Manchester United some eight years earlier. During World War Two, the Old Trafford ground was badly damaged by German bombs and the team played on Manchester City's Maine Road ground at Moss Side until well after the war. The club is now hugely famous and the Old Trafford ground has been developed beyond all recognition to become one of the world's great stadiums.

As Stretford developed into an urban area, land was constantly being lost to housing, and

This photograph of the Old Recreation Ground in School Road, Stretford, was taken in the early 1900s.

the need for parks and open spaces became even more important. One of the first public parks to open in Stretford was on land close to Pinnington Lane, running through to Cyprus Street. Known locally as simply 'the Rec', it was about the size of a football pitch. It opened in 1890 and local celebrations for the coronation of Edward VII were held there in 1902. Eventually this was replaced by Victoria Park, which covered an area of around 19 acres. Other parks in the area were Hullard Park, which stood in the grounds of what was once Hullard Hall and was the first park to be opened by the local authority, Gorse Hill Park and Longford Park, which today occupies land where Longford Hall once stood.

Mr John Rylands, the local entrepreneur who we met in a previous chapter, was responsible for building the first public baths around 1885. They were situated on Dorset Street and were about 22ft in length. Facilities were very different from modern pools and male and female bathers were not allowed to bathe on the same days; prices were higher on days when the water was changed. Admission prices ranged from 4d on 'clean' days, reducing to 2d on other days. In 1909 the local authority purchased the baths and in 1912 carried out extensive alterations, adding another swimming bath, this one measuring 75ft in length. In 1904, two other swimming baths had been opened in Old Trafford, and in 1928 a swimming bath was opened in Trafford Park.

Many forms of entertainment still relied on the church and local bands. Drama groups and meetings often met in church halls throughout

Children playing in Gorse Hill Park during the summer of 1951.

Stretford. In November 1907 a potato pie supper was held at St Peter's Church, and, at Stretford Lecture Hall, a floral service was held with prizes for the best entries.

Cinema became very popular during the early part of 20th century, providing a new form of entertainment and an escape from the drudgery of working life. The Picturedrome, which was situated on King Street, was one of the first cinemas in Stretford. The 900-seat Corona cinema on Moss Road, which was opened in 1929, was one of the first cinemas to show talking pictures. The Longford Theatre, opened in October 1936, was the work of Mr Henry Elder, who was responsible for its unique design. In August 1950 it was renamed the Essoldo and, during the 1960s, was used as bingo hall.

Although the building stands empty at the time of writing, it remains a prominent Stretford landmark. In Old Trafford there was the Globe cinema on Cornbrook Street and the Trafford on Chorlton Road.

Stretford pageant is one annual festival that continues to this day, taking place during July. The pageant begins with a procession through the streets of Stretford, culminating in the crowning of the Rose Queen in Longford Park. The procession, which consists of brightly decorated floats, can be traced back to 1919 when the festival was inaugurated. The tradition of the Rose Queen, however, dates from slightly earlier in 1909 when a 'queen' was chosen by members of St Peter's Church and crowned at a festival held at Gorse Hill Farm.

In 1844, Pomona Gardens regatta involved boat races up and down the River Irwell. It is hard to imagine that this area of Stretford was once a local beauty spot and provided a lovely venue for an afternoon out. The grandstand, which can be seen on the left of the picture, is where the Manchester Docks are now situated.

The boathouse of the Nemesis Rowing Club. The boathouse, built in 1850, was situated on the banks of the River Irwell. It was demolished in 1890 to accommodate the building of the Manchester Ship Canal. The building, which can be seen on the right is that of the Pomona Palace which measured 45,800sq ft and was said to hold 28,000 people.

Stretford Baths in Cyprus Street were opened to the public on 10 May 1913.

Slipper baths were once a common feature in public baths providing a much-needed place bathing for the many people who lived in older houses which did not have a bathroom, and usually had an outside lavatory. The local authority provided both bathing and laundry facilities, where clothes could be taken for washing. This is Old Trafford slipper baths in 1958.

The Corona cinema was built in Moss Road in 1930. When it closed in 1951 there was a scheme to turn it into a theatre, but the idea was eventually dropped. The site became a car park for Metropolitan-Vickers instead.

John Rylands was responsible for establishing the first free public lending library in Stretford in 1883, but after his death 10 years later, this responsibility transferred to the local authority. The library service continued to expand with Old Trafford library being built in 1901, Trafford Park library in 1904, and Firswood and Lostock libraries established during the 1930s. This is Firswood library in 1938.

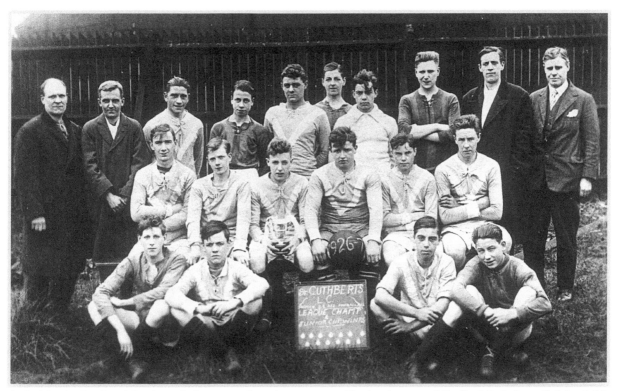

St Cuthbert's, Sunday School Football League champions 1926–7. The headmaster of Trafford Park Council School, Mr Baker, can be seen on the far right of the back row.

The 1st Longford Boy Scouts troop were founded in 1908 by Mr W.E. Gregson. The Scouts held their first meetings in the Union Church. In 1911 they were honoured by a visit from the founder of the Boy Scouts movement, Sir Robert Baden Powell, who was later enobled. The Scouts are seen here in 1910, during a stay at their camp in Leigh.

Boy Scouts camping in Trafford Park c.1900.

The Botanical Gardens played host to the Art Treasures Exhibition in 1857, which was attended by Queen Victoria and Prince Albert and was considered a great success.

The 'Red Indians' pictured here were taking part in the Buffalo Bill Wild West Show which toured England during 1887. The show, which portrayed life in the Wild West, visited Stretford's Botanical Gardens on two occasions. The entertainment included daring horse-riding displays, mock battles and hand-to-hand combat between the Cowboys and Indians. The show was run by Buffalo Bill himself, Colonel William F. Cody. For a time the Indians lodged at Salford and during their stay Edward Little Chief – a grandson of Sitting Bull – of the Ogallala band of the Dakota Sioux, and his wife, Good Robe, had their daughter, Frances Victoria Alexandra, baptised at St Clement's Church in Salford.

The Samuel Brooks stand at the 1887 Royal Jubilee Exhibition at Old Trafford.

The Royal Jubilee Exhibition was staged at Old Trafford in 1887. This view of the grounds shows the basin of the Fairy Fountain, the lake and church.

The Scenic Railway continued in use after the Royal Jubilee Exhibition closed. The ride was noisy and a local newspaper received complaints that the noise from the revellers could be heard in local schools and distracted pupils from their work. with the Industrial Design stand, below.

Lancashire County Cricket Club started out in 1817 as Manchester Cricket Club. The club's first grounds were at Salford, then Hulme before they moved to a ground behind the Botanical Gardens. When that site was required for the Art Treasures Exhibition in 1857, the club moved to new premises on Warwick Road where it has stayed ever since and which is known throughout the cricket world simply as Old Trafford.

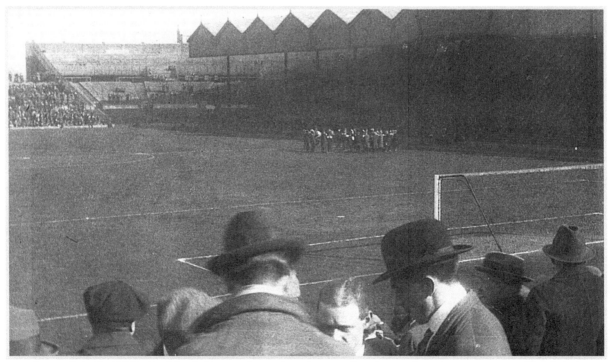

Manchester United's Old Trafford football ground, seen here in 1927, is a far cry from the spectacular self-styled Theatre of Dreams of today. Football was originally a male-dominated sport and few women attended matches, as can be seen from this photograph.

An aerial view of Manchester United's Old Trafford football ground in 1969.

IN TIMES OF CONFLICT

THROUGHOUT history, Stretford has been touched by many of the conflicts which have affected Britain. After the Romans invaded Britain in AD 43, they subsequently marched northwards and surely passed through the district by what became one of their main roads, from Chester to Manchester via a ford at the site of Crossford Bridge. Although no documentation exists to confirm the possibility, it seems likely that they reached Manchester, where they established a fort, along this road.

Then, in the Chetham Library, there is a Muster Role for 1569, giving the names of about 900 local men able to bear arms. The roll consists of several pieces of paper sewn together and is several yards long.

In the English Civil War, troops also crossed this ford on their way to Manchester, and in 1745, when Bonnie Prince Charlie was marching south, the bridge that had been built to replace the ford was demolished, on government orders, to stop the rebels. On his departure from Manchester on 30 November 1745, a proclamation was issued: 'His Royal Highness being informed that several bridges have been pulled down in the county, he has given orders to repair them forthwith, particularly that at Crossford, which is to be done by his own troops, though His Royal Highness does not propose to make use of it for his own army, but believes it will be of service to the country and if any forces that are with General Wade be coming this road they may have benefit of it.'

The Manchester constable's accounts for November 1745 report that £2 9s 0d was paid to Sunday labour 'forced this day by the rebels to Crossford Bridge' and £1 8s 5d paid for a drink for them at Stretford. In the event, the Young Pretender's main army did not use this route, but it is thought that a party of 200 passed over the river here to join the main army at Macclesfield.

Stretford men are known to have served in the Napoleonic Wars. It is said that some of them were press-ganged, which is not surprising as this was a common way of recruiting men. In Trafford's Local History Collection there are copies of letters and accounts from two seamen, Samuel Hampson and Joseph Hulme, who served on HMS *Athenian* and HMS *Puissant*, respectively, to their families in Stretford and which give some idea of their lives on board.

Although there is little documentation on Stretford concerning World War One, the community played its part with enthusiasm. In Stretford, just as in every town and village across the land, men volunteered in great numbers to fight for King and Country. And like every other community, Stretford lost many of its finest young citizens. Some 400–500 local men died in the conflict and many more were severely injured. The appalling conditions of life on the Western Front, in particular, are well-documented, but it is doubtful that any could have imagined what horrors lay ahead as they crowded into local recruiting offices on a wave of patriotic fervour.

The men served in a wide variety of regiments – the Manchester Regiment, the Lancashire Fusiliers, the Royal Engineers, the King's Own Scottish Borderers, the Rifle Brigade and the Grenadier Guards to name but a few. A few joined the newly-formed Royal Flying Corps, and at least six local men were lost at sea, including Captain Carleton Barnett of the troopship *Stuart Prince*.

Besides those who died, or were badly injured, many others served valiantly in the war. One such was 29-year-old Harry Coverdale, who lived in Skerton Street and before the war had worked as an engineer at Galloway's boiler works in Knott Mill. He enlisted in the Manchester Regiment and first served in the Gallipoli campaign. Then he was posted to the Western Front and on 4 October 1917, he was awarded the Victoria Cross for conspicuous bravery in an attack on enemy strongholds south-west of Poelcapelle, near Passchendaele, Belgium.

The official citation reads in part: '...Sergeant Coverdale disposed of three snipers. He then rushed two machine guns, killing or wounding the teams. He subsequently reorganised his platoon in order to capture another position, but after getting to within 100 yards of it was held back by our own barrage and had to return. Later he went out again with five men to capture

Concert party organised by soldiers at the Victoria Park Military Hospital during World War One. Victoria Park Council School was placed at the disposal of the Red Cross and within 12 days the premises were converted from a school with 800 pupils to a 120-bed hospital, later to be increased to 230. There were 18 wards, an operating theatre, two recreation rooms, a billiard room and offices.

The Drumhead Service, Longford Park, 26 September 1915. This service was held to raise spirits and money for the war effort, and consisted of hymns and an address or sermon. As can be seen here it was well attended by both dignitaries and the local population. The ceremony was to be repeated in World War Two.

Company Sergeant Frank Munday of the 7th Battalion, Manchester Regiment, who died of his wounds received in action in the Dardenelles on 4 June 1915. He was previously the caretaker of Seymour Park Council School.

the position, but when he saw a considerable number of the enemy advancing, withdrew his detachment, man by man, he himself being the last to retire.' Harry Coverdale, who also received the Military Medal, left the army with the rank of second-lieutenant. He died in Huddersfield in 1955.

In 1919, Stretford Council made a public appeal for subscriptions to fund a suitable war memorial. In all, £9,274 was raised, £6,000 of which was contributed by the Stretford Red Cross Society and £3,274 by the public. The council decided that the money should be spent on establishing a district nursing service,

In April 1918, Councillor Finney, Chairman of Stretford Urban District Council, makes a presentation to Second-Lieutenant Harry Coverdale, who received the Victoria Cross, the highest gallantry honour.

The Victory Ball of 1919 was to celebrate the end of World War One the previous year. The theme was fancy dress and included an array of different costumes. The ball was held in the Civic Theatre.

administered by trustees representing the Stretford Red Cross Society and Stretford Council, and a memorial, costing £2,000, be placed on Chester Road. The land on which the memorial was to be built was given by the de Trafford trustees as a permanent open space.

During the war, the Stretford Red Cross Society had been responsible for the upkeep and running of hospitals at the County Cricket Ground and at the Victoria Park School, and the money allocated to them enabled them to provide three district nurses until the service was taken over by Lancashire County Council under the Public Health Act in 1948. The founding of

Stretford Memorial Hospital was possible due to a trust established at this time, together with a gift of £500 from George V's Silver Jubilee Fund, together with support from Stretford pageant. Basford House on Seymour Grove had been used as an auxiliary hospital during the war, accommodating 30 patients. The Memorial Trust eventually bought the house and thus Stretford Memorial Hospital was born. Trafford Hall was also used as a hospital, the whole of the equipment being provided by Trafford Park Estate Company. The grounds and the lake were a great attraction to the patients and staff, the latter being lent a private car by the Ford com-

Stretford Cenotaph pictured in 1923. The £2,000 cost of the memorial was donated after World War One by the Red Cross and members of the public. The monument is in cenotaph form on a base with three steps and a moulded plinth showing in raised figures the dates of war. It is 24ft high and 11ft wide and the Stretford coat-of-arms is displayed on carved shields. The surround wall is semi-circular and made of Derbyshire stone, with a curved bronze tablet containing the names and regiments of the fallen. The memorial is sited opposite the Chester Road entrance to Gorse Hill Park. It was unveiled on 25 April 1923 by the Earl of Derby, who was then Secretary of State for War.

pany, with petrol and a chauffeur.

At the cessation of war, Stretford celebrated in style. In 1919, a victory ball was held at the Town Hall and a peace festival was organised in Longford Park in July of the same year, the highlight of which was a grand firework display.

While many had lost husbands, fathers, brothers, close friends and neighbours during World War One, the local population had been in little immediate danger as aerial bombardment was in its infancy. However, life during World War Two was to prove quite different. Stretford, in the middle of a hugely important industrial area, was to be the target of much heavy bombing. Although tension in Europe had been building throughout the summer, after war was declared on 3 September 1939, there followed a six-month so-called 'Phoney War'. Enemy aircraft were occasionally seen overhead, but there was no real hint of what was to come. Stretford, like the rest of Britain, simply watched, waited and prepared.

One measure was the evacuation of local children to various 'safer' places. Two hundred children from Victoria Park School were sent to Lymm, and the children from Longford School

In 1938 the German Luftwaffe had flown across Britain on 'goodwill flights' and built up an extensive archive of aerial photographs of the country. As can be seen from this annotated Ordnance Survey map of Salford and Stretford, when war was declared the following year, the Nazis already possessed much detailed information about important industrial sites and access routes.

DESTITUTION

Temporary

If inquirer is in need of financial help as a result of a raid, he may apply to the Assistance Board Officer at the Rest Centre, or at Area Office, Dover Street Schools, Chorlton-on-Medlock, Manchester, for Local Office, see ADDRESSES: if already billeted by the Council to the Employment Exchange, Church Hall, Market Street, Stretford, for Stretford, Trafford Park and Old Trafford as far as Seymour Grove; 109 Princess Street, Manchester (off Whitworth Street) or St. Stephen's Schools, City Road, for the rest of Old Trafford, taking with him his billeting certificate.

If inquirer is a pensioner and is now some distance from his usual Post Office he may draw his pension from the nearest Office.

LOCAL FUNDS

The Air Raid Distress Fund is administered from the Town Hall by His Worship the Mayor. The Fund is designed to assist those persons who are in need through the effects of enemy action and who are not eligible for the grants or allowances made by the Public Assistance Committee or Assistance Board.

see also Household Effects

EVACUATION

OFFICIAL ARRANGEMENTS.

Evacuation is possible at all times and School Children can usually be evacuated in parties accompanied by teachers within a few days of being registered.

Expectant Mothers may register for evacuation. They will be evacuated when they are within one month of confinement. Inquires may be made to nearest Child Welfare Centre, Municipal Midwives, or Health Department, Room 5, Ground Floor, Town Hall.

PRIVATE ARRANGEMENTS

Persons who can make private arrangements with householders elsewhere, can, if they are in either of the following classes (a or b), get free travel vouchers and billeting certificates from the Evacuation Office, Room 15, Ground Floor;

12

Town Hall. Persons in class (c) apply to the Billeting Officer Ground Floor, Town Hall.

Billeting allowances will be paid through the Billeting Officer of the new district, to the householders with whom they stay.

(a) Unaccompanied school children may go to a reception or a neutral area. Billeting allowances will be paid if it is clear that the child cannot be maintained without hardship.

(b) Mothers with children of school age or under.

(c) Aged, infirm or invalid persons, blind persons and expectant mothers.

BILLETING ALLOWANCES

For unaccompanied children, under official arrangements, the rates vary from 8s. 6d. to 15s. per week according to age, and provide for board and lodging. For adults the rate is 5s. per week and for children under 14, accompanied by adults, 3s. per week; each amount providing for lodging only. If inquirer has not enough money to buy food and other necessities he may apply to the Office of the Assistance Board in the place where he is billeted. The Billeting Officer will tell him where this office is. Parents of unaccompanied school children may be asked to contribute towards the cost of board and lodging.

NOTES

The value of free travel permits is not recoverable. Billeting fees are recoverable from parents of unaccompanied children, if the financial position of the parents permits such recovery.

Billeting fees are recoverable from expectant mothers evacuated by the Health Department, but such recovery is dependent upon the circumstances of the mother.

FOOD SUPPLIES

If a shop dealing in rationed Food Stuffs ceases business, its registered customers should take their ration books at once to the Food Office, 104 Talbot Road, Old Trafford, where one of the following arrangements will be made for them:—

(1) If the shopkeeper is likely to resume business within a few days an Emergency Ration Card will be issued allowing one week's rations to be purchased at the nearest available shop in the Borough.

13

Air-raid advice notes were designed to help the general public in a number of way such as, shown here, the arrangements which could be made for the evacuation of children to areas less threatened by air-raids.

went to Ashley. Although these areas were not far away, they did not face the same threat which industrialised Stretford, with its Trafford Park, did. Stretford Boys Grammar School and Stretford High School for Girls had both been evacuated to Macclesfield immediately prior to the outbreak of war and Company 202 of the Manchester Regiment took over the boys' school.

But the Phoney War dragged on and slowly, the children began to return, the threat seemingly past. In May 1940, however, the Germans invaded France and the Low Countries. An invasion of Britain seemed imminent, air-raids now a certainty, and once more the children were sent away to safer pastures. They were not always happy in their new homes. A.J. Atherton, in his diaries of the war years, talks of the dentist and his wife with whom he was billeted as a 'distant and unemotional pair who made it quite clear to us from the start that they were obliged to take us in only because they had spare room... we were never to use the front door, never to use any other rooms and to keep to the back of the house.'

It must have been traumatic for families to be separated, especially as, sometimes, mothers didn't know where their children – some of whom were very young – were going.

Before long, air-raids began in earnest. Air-

ADDRESSES

Town Hall	Talbot Road, Stretford ... ... TRA 2101
Addresses, changed ...	Citizens' Advice Bureaux; each Public Library.
Air Raid Distress Fund	The Mayor, Town Hall.
A.R. Wardens' Headquarters	841 Chester Road, Stretford ... ... LON 1006
Assistance Board	Warwick House, Ashton Lane, Sale ...SAL 4286-7
Local Office	Town Hall ... ... TRA 2101
	The Local Office will be open as required by conditions. Hours of opening may be obtained from Information Centre.
Billeting Officer	General inquiries, 100 Talbot Road ... TRA 1680 -1689
Borough Surveyor ...	General inquiries, Room 7, First Floor, Town Hall.
Casualty Inquiries ...	98 Talbot Road ... ... TRA 1968
Casualty Lists	Displayed at :— Police Stations Public Libraries Town Hall
Cemetery Registrar ...	Cemetery, Lime Road, Stretford ... LON 1425
Citizens' Advice Bureaux	Each Public Library in Borough :—
	Old Trafford ... ... TRA 1332 -2639
	Stretford ... ... LON 1063
	Firswood ... ... CHO 2709
	Lostock ... ... LON 1710
	Trafford Park ... ... TRA 1108
	and after severe air raids :— Entrance Hall, Town Hall.
Civil Defence Office ...	98 Talbot Road ... ... TRA 1968
Civil Defence Recruiting	
Air Raid Wardens ...	841 Chester Road ... ... LON 1096
Ambulance and First Aid	Medical Officer of Health, Room 5, Ground Floor Town Hall ... ...
Fire Guard...	841 Chester Road ... ... LON 1598
Messenger Service ...	Civil Defence Office, 98 Talbot Road, or at above offices for special services.
Special Constabulary	Superintendent of Police, Old Trafford ; Northwood, Seymour Grove ... ... TRA 2150
Claim Forms for Damage	Room 30, First Floor, Town Hall, and Citizens' Advice Bureaux.
Commercial Inquiries ...	Manchester Chamber of Commerce, Ship Canal House, King Street, Manchester, 2 ... ... DEA 5574
Customs and Excise ...	56 Talbot Road, Old Trafford ... ... TRA 1908

6

Damage to Property :—	
First Aid Repairs ...	Room 7, First Floor, Town Hall.
Repairs, Claims and Payments	War Damages Commission, Lancaster House, Whitworth, Street, Manchester ... ... CEN 5657
District Valuer	Room 81, Fourth Floor, Sunlight House, Quay Street, Manchester, 3 BLA 8200
Education Inquiries ...	Room 12, First Floor, Town Hall.
Electricity Inquiries ...	Stretford & District Electricity Board, Longford Bridge, Chester Road ... LON 2461
	Trafford Park ... ... TRA 0431
	Manchester ... ... CEN 3211
	During Raids ... ... CEN 0083
Employment Exchanges	Stretford (Men)—Church Hall, Market Street ... ... LON 2453
	(Women)—Brunswick Street ... ... LON 2419
	National Service Officer, Market St. LON 2453
	Old Trafford : 109 Princess Street, Manchester, 1 ... ... CEN 2901
Evacuation Officer ...	Room 15, Ground Floor, Town Hall ...
Fire Brigade	Park Road, Stretford—
	Fire calls ... ... LON 2222
	Business calls ... ... LON 2424
Fire Guard Office ...	841 Chester Road ... ... LON 1598
First Aid Posts	Child Welfare Clinic, Mitford Street, Stretford ... ... LON 1016
	Seymour Park School, Northumberland Road, Old Trafford ... ... TRA 1149
	Trafford Park School, Trafford Park ... TRA 0531
Food Inspector	Room 6, Ground Floor, Town Hall.
Food Office	104 Talbot Road, Old Trafford TRA 0887-8
Funeral Arrangements (Public)	98 Talbot Road ... ... TRA 1968
Furniture Removal ...	Room 7, First Floor, Town Hall.
Gas Decontamination Centres	Unwounded members of public :— Victoria Park Schools Gorse Hill School Old Trafford Baths (later) Civil Defence Personnel and Home Guard :—Stretford Baths.
Gas Inquiries	Stretford : Stretford & District Gas Board, Longford Road ... ... LON 1133
	Old Trafford : Gas Department, Town Hall, Manchester, 2 ... ... CEN 3377
	Street Mains : Gaythorn, Manchester. CEN 0441
Information Centre ...	Public Library, Old Trafford ... ... TRA 1332 -2639
	After severe raids—Entrance Hall, Town Hall.

7

Part of a Civil Defence booklet which showed the addresses of local services, ranging from casualty lists to Customs and Excise enquiries, from public funerals to claims for damage caused by the bombing.

raid shelters had been erected both in homes and in shopping areas, and public buildings had been sandbagged. First-aid posts were set up at Mitford Street and Northumberland Road and a mobile first-aid unit was launched. Minor injuries were treated at these posts, while more serious cases were sent to Nell Lane Hospital. Records of people injured or killed were posted in public libraries and at the Town Hall. Gas decontamination centres were also set up, for both the general public and the Civil Defence, which included police, rescue and ambulance services. There were numerous air-raid wardens' (ARP) posts and volunteers were hastily recruited for this job. Rest centres provided food and shelter for those unfortunate souls whose

homes had been destroyed or had become uninhabitable, and an Air Raid Distress Fund was also available for the destitute.

As the threat of invasion mounted, in Stretford two units of the Local Defence Volunteers (soon to be renamed the Home Guard) were formed. Civilians were encouraged to volunteer and many, who were either too young or too old to serve in the military, took the opportunity to do do their bit after work. Their job was to patrol the area and protect vital installations. 'A' Company controlled the area from Old Trafford to Longford Bridge, their headquarters being on Seymour Grove, and 'D' Company controlled the rest of Stretford, their headquarters being on Edge Lane. Both these companies were part of

The Mayor and Mayoress, Councillor and Mrs Willoughby, present an ambulance to First-aid post No.1 in August 1941 and below, First-aid post No.1, showing cars and personnel. The man wearing a tin hat, in the middle of the centre group, is George Shawcross, an ambulance driver. This first-aid post was situated at the Child Care Clinic on Mitford Street and the attending medical officer was Dr W. Westwood. People with less serious injuries would be dealt with here, and others more badly injured were referred to hospital. The ambulances were driven by volunteers and carried ambulance attendants.

First-aid post No. 2 personnel on exercise at Seymour Park School. The FAPs were manned by both auxiliary and full-time nurses, the former working all day in hospitals and then two or three nights a week at their post. The staff were given first-aid training with regular examinations to test their knowledge. The medical officers here were Dr Isbister and Dr Weatherhead.

the 44th Battalion which covered Stretford, Urmston, Flixton and Davyhulme. There were six guardrooms in Stretford – on Stamford Street, Northumberland Road, Cromwell Street, Chester Road, Derbyshire Lane and Market Street. Volunteers were issued with khaki uniforms and eventually with rifles, although at first broomsticks were used for training. They had regular training sessions on local fields. One particularly important point of defence – as it had been so many times in the past – was Crossford Bridge where, between shifts, the guards slept in the cellar of the Bridge Inn.

Another feature of wartime Stretford was the placing of barrage balloons. These were manned by RAF balloon barrage squadrons and the balloons were used to protect the area from low-flying aircraft. The 924, 925, and 926 Squadrons were formed to protect Stretford, Eccles and parts of Salford including the docks and Trafford Park. Volunteers had begun their training in 1939, at the old Manchester Grammar School in Long Millgate. They were trained by regular RAF instructors and their headquarters were at the Salisbury Hotel on Trafford Road. Balloons were moored all over the area, including Seymour Grove, Victoria Park, Lostock, Warwick Road, Park Road and No 9 Dock of the Manchester Ship Canal. Maintaining these balloons was a skilled job because they had to be monitored 24

Nurses outside and the sandbagged First-aid post No. 2 at Seymour Park School.

hours a day to ensure they didn't break their moorings, and the balloons had to be hauled down in bad weather. They must have been a strange sight, but their presence did much to reassure the public.

Because of what was deemed a realistic threat of a Nazi invasion, in 1941 the Civil Defence issued a booklet outlining what their role would be should church bells be rung to warn that the invasion had started. This, of course, included keeping the population indoors, but it also required the destruction of all maps, and many other measures to slow down the enemy advance. Already, many roadside directional signs had been removed, and buses no longer showed their destinations. Railway stations, included Stretford, saw their name signs

removed. Bicycles and motor vehicles had to be immobilised when not in use and it was a criminal offence not to comply with that order.

As the war progressed, commodities became scarcer. Fuel had already been rationed and in October 1939, as fresh foods became less available, a local Dig for Victory campaign was launched in line with the rest of the country. The playing fields in Moss Park were utilised, as were parts of Longford Park, Trafford Park and Old Trafford. People were encouraged to dig up their gardens and all sorts of produce was grown including onions, which were in very short supply. Once-prized front lawns became vegetable patches.

Stretford was to receive two visits from King George VI and Queen Elizabeth. On Thursday 2

The presentation of ambulances to the council. These vehicles were formerly Kellogg's delivery vans. The ambulance service relied heavily on donations from individuals as well as companies providing and equipping the vehicles.

Stretford Girls' High School pictured here in June 1935. In December 1940 the school was extensively damaged by enemy action and was later demolished.

St Hilda's Church, Old Trafford, showing bomb damage.

All Saints' Church, Cyprus Street, Stretford, was hit by an incendiary on 23 December 1940.

May 1940, the couple visited Metropolitan-Vickers in Trafford Park. Thousands of workers cheered them as they inspected the works and spoke to fire service, Civil Defence volunteers and Red Cross nurses. Since 1938, 'Metrovicks' had been working on the production of a jet-propelled aircraft and they were also responsible for the production of the first Manchester bomber, which was destroyed by a direct hit on the factory in December 1940. One dozen others were also destroyed but, despite this, in less than four weeks production was running at 80% capacity. On 13 February 1941, the King and Queen visited the factory again and also went to Old Trafford Senior Boys School.

Stretford suffered its most severe bomb damage during the blitz in December 1940. When Metrovicks was hit, burning chemicals blackened the whole sky. A gas main was hit in

King's Road and the resulting fire acted as a beacon for further bombing. Of course, Trafford Park was the main target, but the surrounding area took some devastating blows. Old Trafford Baths was hit and St Peter's School, Gorse Hill, and the Royal School for the Deaf were partially destroyed. Stretford High School for Girls was hit by a landmine, and incendiary bombs landed all around the area, falling on Quick's Garage on Chester Road, the Globe cinema and the gasworks. High-explosive bombs landed on Cornbrook Road, Derbyshire Avenue and Milton Road – from where 40 people were evacuated – and Ryebank Road, where a water mains was burst. The Town Hall was hit on 23 December, and 200 people in Barlow Road had a lucky escape when a bomb fell but did not explode. A total of 124 incendiary bombs and 120 high-

The Mayor inspects a parade of air-raid wardens in November 1940.

explosive bombs fell on 22 and 23 December, killing a total of 73 people with many more injured.

Manchester United's Old Trafford football ground was badly hit during an air-raid on 11 March 1941, and an estimated £50,000 damage was done. The main stand was completely burned out, the pitch and parts of the terracing badly scorched, and much equipment was lost. The damage was so bad that the club were unable to return until August 1949. They were probably the worst-hit of all Football League clubs during World War Two, and were awarded £22,278 by the War Damage Commission, to clear away the debris and rebuild the ground. A massive 120,000-capacity stadium was planned but financial restrictions prevented it and in the end only the main stand was rebuilt.

Amazingly, the spirit of the people of Stretford was by no means daunted by these terrible events as death rained down from the sky. In 1941, Stretford's War Weapons Week aimed to raise £500,000. In March 1942, Warship Week was held to raise the £400,000 needed for Stretford to adopt HMS *Escapade*. Wings for Victory Week took place on 8–15 May 1943, when the people of Stretford hoped to raise enough money to build and equip 12 Lancaster

On 13 February 1941, George VI and Queen Elizabeth visited Stretford. Here, the Queen alights from her car.

bombers. In 1944, Salute the Soldier Week was launched, this time for weapons and uniforms for serving soldiers.

The war in Europe ended in May 1945 and Stretford, along with the rest of the country, celebrated VE Day. Three months later, following the atomic bombs on Hiroshima and Nagasaki, Japan surrendered and in Stretford, VJ Day was celebrated as heartily as anywhere. After the announcement of peace, over 20,000 people congregated on open spaces, dancing to gramophone music to the early hours. Although fireworks were in short supply, several bonfires were lit, and fairylights were put up in Longford

King George VI, with his back to the camera, and Queen Elizabeth, accompanied by the Mayor and Mayoress, meet members of local Home Guard. Also on parade are fire brigade personnel.

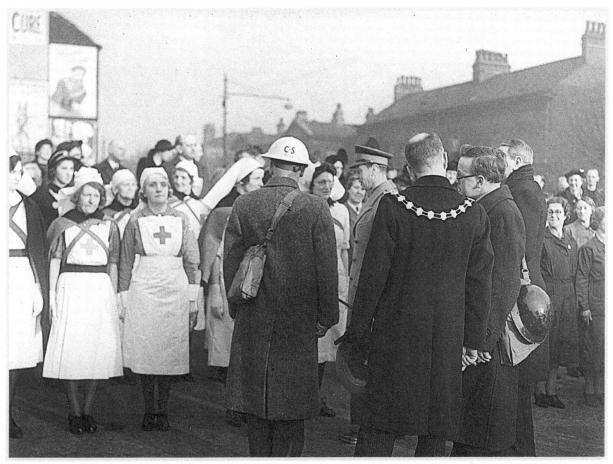

Red Cross Nurses meet the King at Old Trafford Senior Boys' School during the royal visit. Dr W. Westwood is wearing the white 'tin hat'. The Mayor is talking to Herbert Morrison MP.

Park Many communities held street parties, and public buildings were floodlit in a dramatic display of joy after so many years of nightly blackouts. Of course, these celebrations were tinged with sadness for those whose friends and family members would not return home. But there was hope that these brave men had not died in vain and that this war really would be the end to all fighting.

King George VI inspects the Special Police while the Queen chats with local officials.

The royal couple leaving Old Trafford Senior Boys' School.

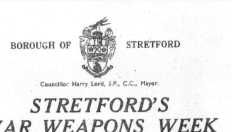

BOROUGH OF STRETFORD

Councillor Harry Lord, J.P., C.C., Mayor.

STRETFORD'S WAR WEAPONS WEEK

May 10th to May 17th, 1941.

Town Hall,
Stretford.
May, 1941.

Stretford has had its share of attention from the Enemies of Civilisation, and the most effective way in which we ordinary folk can retaliate, is by making our War Weapons Week an unqualified success.

This is our chance to show that we are prepared to go to the extreme limit of our respective resources to make certain that our fighting men are supplied with the essentials for carrying on the struggle with those who are threatening us with the loss of all that we hold dear.

Having regard to the results obtained in the neighbouring areas our aim of:—

£500,000

should be easily capable of achievement, and we are confident that you will rise to the occasion.

An attractive programme of events has been arranged for the week, details of which you will find in the following pages, and we ask your support in making each day a success.

The attention of the Ladies of the Borough is particularly called to the meeting in Longford Park on Wednesday, when MISS ELLEN WILKINSON, M.P., will speak, and also to Thursday, which day is being organised entirely by the Ladies. Help them to help our boys.

The visit of LORD DERBY on the final day will provide a fitting climax to a week of combined effort, which should be long remembered with satisfaction and pride as the week when we in Stretford went—

ALL OUT — ALL OF US — ALL THE TIME.

HARRY LORD, Mayor.
WALTER THORPE,
Chairman of Local Savings Committee.
CHAS. TREWAVAS,
Hon. Secretary, Local Savings Committee.

Leaflet advertising Stretford's War Weapons Week in May 1941. The event began with an exhibition in the public hall, displaying guns, parachutes and a petrol bomb which was 6ft long. There were also parades, a children's day and ladies' day which hosted a whist drive and bring-and-buy sale.

Part of the parade in Longford Park during War Weapons Week, May 1941. The Mayor, Councillor Lord, and the mace bearer watch a military band. In the background appear to be members of the Home Guard.

A naval unit is inspected by the Mayor on Longford Park during War Weapons Week.

Radio comedy pair Elsie and Doris Waters line up for a cup of tea at a mobile canteen during War Weapons Week. Also pictured (left to right) are Miss Bagley, Mrs Willoughby, Mrs Lord, Councillor Lord (the Mayor), Councillor Willoughby (Deputy Mayor), an unidentified tea lady and Councillor Mrs Bagley. Elsie and Doris Waters were famous throughout Britain for their radio performances and were the sisters of Jack Warner, another famous radio name during the war, who went on to enjoy even greater fame in BBC television's *Dixon of Dock Green*.

Members of the Auxiliary Fire Service drive past at Longford Park during War Weapons Week.

Air-raid wardens at Longford Park in May 1941. The wardens played a vital role during the bombing.

Members of the Women's Auxiliary Air Force (WAAF) marching in Longford Park, May 1941.

Rescue and decontamination squads, so vital during the blitz on Stretford, take their turn in the limelight during War Weapons Week.

At the end of War Weapons Week, Lord Derby visited Stretford and gave a speech in Longford Park.

War Weapons Week, May 1941. The Mayor, Councillor Lord, indicates the total so far collected. As we can see, the target of £500,000 has already been met.

Air Training Corps members parading at Stretford pageant in 1942. The RAF required many more personnel during the war and the ATC trained young men over the age of 16 who wanted to enter either the Royal Air Force or the Royal Naval Air Service. Lord Derby is watching the march past.

WEDNESDAY, MARCH 18th

11 a.m to 8 p.m.

LADIES' FAIR at Stretford Public Hall

Organised by Street Groups Sub-Committee.

THURSDAY, MARCH 19th

WOMENS' DAY

The investments made on this day will be credited to the Ladies who are making a special effort to achieve the maximum result, and appeal for the support of all women to make the day an outstanding success.

7-30 p.m. THE MANHATTAN CONCERT PARTY

will give a performance in

THE STRETFORD PUBLIC HALL.

Organised by the Gorse Hill National Savings Secretaries.

Tickets of Admission 1/- and 1/6. Children half-price.

SATURDAY, MARCH 21st

7 to 11 p.m.

WARSHIP WEEK DANCE AT THE STRETFORD TECHNICAL COLLEGE

A fitting finale to a campaign of great endeavour.

Music by TED HARGREAVES AND HIS ORCHESTRA.

A Mobile Selling Centre

will tour the Borough each day (except Sunday) from 5 p.m. to 8 p.m. for the convenience of those who are unable to visit the fixed Selling Centres.

The net Proceeds from the various Concerts, Efforts and Collections taken during the week, after deducting the expenses of the campaign, will be invested in War Bonds for the KING GEORGE'S FUND FOR SAILORS WAR FUND which benefits Sailors of all kinds who are risking their lives for us in this Great War. LET US SHOW HOW MUCH WE APPRECIATE THE GRAND WORK THEY ARE DOING.

BOROUGH OF  STRETFORD

Councillor Lady Robinson, J.P., Mayor.

STRETFORD'S WARSHIP WEEK

March 14th to March 21st, 1942.

Town Hall,
Stretford,
March, 1942.

The Stretford Local Savings Committee has set itself the task of securing the investment in Stretford during Warship Week of at least

£400,000

This is the sum required for the building of a Destroyer of the "Hunt" Class, and if the target is reached, Stretford will be able to adopt H.M.S. "ESCAPADE" a ship of that class.

I appeal to all who live or work in the Borough to do their utmost to help in providing the wherewithal to supply the nation's need for more and yet more warships, a need which recent events in the Far East and elsewhere have so strongly emphasised.

I am confident that Stretford can be relied upon to play its part in this campaign, as it is doing in so many other directions, so that the War may be brought to a speedy and successful conclusion.

E. M. ROBINSON,
Mayor.

A leaflet publicising Stretford's Warship Week in March 1942. A salute was taken by Flight-Lieutenant Ralph Etherton MP and there was a public meeting at Stretford Public Hall where the Admiral of the Fleet, Sir Roger Keyes, addressed the people.

Admiral of the Fleet, Sir Roger Keyes, with the Mayor, Councillor Lady Robinson, on the steps of the Town Hall during Warships Week.

The new WVS tea van behind Stretford Town Hall. The anti-incendiary device on the roof in the background can just be seen.

Ingleby, a large house opposite the entrance to Longford Park on Edge Lane, was used as the Auxiliary Fire Service's headquarters. It belonged to Mr Frank Hulme, until his death in 1939, and was a grand house with a staff of several maids, a cook, a gardener and a chauffeur. Note the sandbags piled up against the windows. The make-do fire engine is rather elegant, despite the ladders roped to the roof. The firefighters used water from large tanks situated throughout the area with the letters EWS (emergency water supply) painted on them. They held approximately 10,000 gallons of water and were not covered, which made them a potential safety hazard. The photograph is dated c.1941.

Members of the Women's Junior Air Corps parading at Stretford pageant in March 1943. The corps, which was formed in the early 1940s, originally had its headquarters at Gorse Hill School. The volunteers were taught foot drill by the Home Guard, but membership was few until the Wings for Victory parade in 1943, after which more women volunteered. In this parade 150 women marched and, by then, the WJAC had acquired premises in Seymour Grove. During the war they helped the local balloon barrage squadron and also ran a mobile library. Their name was later to be changed to the Girls' Training Corps and then to the Girls' Adventure Corps Air Cadets.

Representatives of the 4th Indian Division at the Town Hall on 9 October 1943. A formal reception for these visitors was held in the Council Chambers. Only two of the visitors spoke English, so an interpreter was provided. The Indian soldiers visited places of interest in the district including Longford Park and the Metropolitan-Vickers works. They also visited Urmston baths and watched a lifesaving and diving display.

Officers and NCOs of 'D' Company (Stretford) Home Guard, 44th Lancashire Battalion, 1945.

Men and women of Stretford's Civil Defence service pictured towards the end of the war.

Augustus Street, Old Trafford, at 1am on VE Day, 8 May 1945. The cease-fire began at 12.01am on this day and at 3pm the Prime Minister, Winston Churchill, announced the end of the war in Europe. There were special services at local churches, where bells peeled. Here, flags and bunting hang from windows and across the house fronts. Everyone is relieved and happy at the news, although Japan was not to surrender until August 1945. But at least the war against Hitler was over.

On 13 May 1945, a victory thanksgiving service was held at the Longford cinema. A similar service was held in Longford Park on 24 June, the Sunday before the pageant, and the pageant itself staged a victory parade.

The surrender of Japan prompted these headlines in the *Stretford and Urmston News* on Friday 17 August 1945.

MARGARET ELIZABETH BROMILEY.
ELSIE FEATHERSTONE.
EMILY FINCH.
JOHN WILLIAM FINCH.
NORMAN FINCH.
CHARLES GRIFFITHS.
CATHERINE JANE JONES.
FLORENCE JONES.
JAMES JONES.
PATRICIA JONES.
WILLIAM JONES.
KENNETH HAYES.
MABEL HAYES.
MARGARET MARY HAYES.
DIANA HILL.
ANN EVELYN HUGHES.
RAYMOND HUGHES.
FLORENCE MARY HULSON.
VLADIMAR KHARKAVOY.

THIS GARDEN IS DEDICATED TO
THE MEMORY OF THE RESIDENTS
OF STRETFORD. ALSO SEVENTEEN
UNIDENTIFIED PERSONS WHO
LOST THEIR LIVES THROUGH
ENEMY ACTION IN
DECEMBER 1940,
AND WERE INTERRED HERE.

"MAY THEY REST IN PEACE."

ANNIE & GEORGE CLARK.
CATHERINE LAYBOURNE.
GEORGE LAYBOURNE. SR.
GEORGE LAYBOURNE. JR.
JANE LAYBOURNE.
HUGH McLAUGHLIN.
MARY CLAIRE McLAUGHLIN.
MARK McNASH.
ARTHUR WOOD NOBLE.
ARTHUR SIDNEY NORTON.
IRENE NORTON.
JOYCE NORTON.
NELLIE NORTON.
CHRISTOPHER SEAL.
MIRIAM SEAL.
ROBERT SEAL.
GEORGE SKINNER.
NELLIE SMITH.
LEWIS BERTRAM WILKINSON.

On 7 November 1948, this memorial over the communal grave of local air-raid victims was unveiled in Stretford cemetery.

BIBLIOGRAPHY

Atherton, J.G. *Home to Stay* (Neil Richardson, 1991)

Bailey, J. *Old Stretford – a Lecture* (1878)

British Red Cross *Illustrated Account of the Work of the British Red Cross* (Sherratt & Hughes, 1916)

Crofton, H.T. *A History of the Ancient Chapel of Stretford, Vol 1* (Chetham Society, 1898–9)

Crofton, H.T. *A History of the Ancient Chapel of Stretford, Vol 2* (Chetham Society, 1901–2)

Croston, J. *County Families of Lancashire and Cheshire* (John Heywood, 1887)

Geldart, T. *Stretford Congregational Chapel 1829-1921* (City Road Wesleyan Church Grand Jubilee Bazaar, 1911)

Manchester Ship Canal Company *The Bridgewater Canal Company Bicentenary Handbook* (Pyramid Press Ltd)

Massey, S. *A History of Stretford* (Sherratt & Hughes, 1976)

Morrison, Ian and Alan Shury *Manchester United: A Complete Record* (Breedon Books, 1986)

Nicholls, R. *Trafford Park, the First Hundred Years* (Phillimore & Co Ltd, 1996)

Richardson, John *Local Historians' Encyclopedia* (Historical Publications, 1983)

Redhead, M. *Stretford in Times Past* (Countryside Publications, 1979)

Stretford Local History Pack (Trafford MBC)

Stretford Local History Society *Stretford – the Changing Scene*

Taylor, Joyce *The Old Chapel Yard.* (Unpublished manuscript)

Stretford – People and Places (Stretford Local History Society, 1985)

Transactions of the Lancashire and Cheshire Antiquarian Society, 1885

The Police: 150 Years of Policing in the Manchester Area (Archive Publications, 1989)

INDEX

ND - #0236 - 270225 - C0 - 260/195/7 - PB - 9781780914992 - Gloss Lamination